INDIAN POETRY *in* ENGLISH

Edited by
BIRENDRA PANDEY

ATLANTIC

ATLANTIC PUBLISHERS AND DISTRIBUTORS

Published by
ATLANTIC PUBLISHERS AND DISTRIBUTORS
B-2, Vishal Enclave, Opp. Rajouri Garden, New Delhi-27
Phones : 5413460, 5429987
e-mail : info@atlantibooks.com

Sales Office
4215/1, Ansari Road, Darya Ganj, New Delhi-110 002
Phones : 3273880, 3285873, 3280451
Fax : 91-11-3285873
web : www.atlanticbooks.com

ISBN 81-269-0032-6

Typeset at
APD Computer Graphics, Delhi
Printed in India at
Mehra Offset Press, Delhi

To

My Guide

EDITORIAL

This collection of critical essays on contemporary Indian English poetry is my first attempt to explore the worth of individual poets. These poets form the integral part of our national, social and cultural heritage. Many of the poets studied herein have not been able so far to win recognition, but some of them like Keki N. Daruwalla, A.K. Ramanujan, K.R. Srinivasa Iyengar, Niranjan Mohanty and Vikram Seth (also as front-ranking novelists) have received critical perceptives.

In this anthology the essays are the contributions from likeminded scholars from all over the country. They try to follow same critical and analytical style. They have made exhaustive study of the topics they deal with. Though I wanted to include a few women poets but I could not get papers on them. This is the reason that the choice of poets in this anthology is by no means comprehensive. Some relatively new poets have been included while some better known poets have been left out. I am still hopeful of bringing out the second volume on those who have not found place in this volume.

I must put on record my sense of gratitude to those who have enhanced the value of this anthology through their co-operation and words of encouragement, especially to Prof. R.A. Singh, S.P. Jain College, Sasaram (Veer Kunwar Singh University), Prof. O.P. Bhatnagar, Prof. P. Raja, Dr. D.C. Chambial and Dr. P.S. Radha. I am also thankful to my publisher, Dr. K.R. Gupta, Managing Director of M/s Atlantic Publishers and Distributors, New Delhi, for his co-operation at every stage in the preparation of this book.

BIRENDRA PANDEY

CONTENTS

Editorial v

1. East-West Encounter in Indian Poetry in English 1
   —*O.P. Bhatnagar*

2. Daruwalla : A Poet in Search of Identity 16
   —*R.A. Singh*

3. A Ramayana for Women : K.R. Srinivasa Iyengar's *Sitayana* 21
   —*P. Raja*

4. A.K. Ramanujan's "Two Days" : A Stylistic Study 31
   —*G.D. Barche*

5. Soul's Journey in Niranjan Mohanty's *Prayers to Lord Jagannatha* 39
   —*D.C. Chambial*

6. Sailendra Narayan Tripathy's Poetry and his Post-modernist Leanings 50
   —*D. Gnanasekaran*

7. Humour and Irony : A Study of Dr. P. Raja's Poetry 58
   —*K.V. Raghupathi*

8. Vikram Seth's *Beastly Tales* : Humanising Beasts... Beastising Humans 75
   —*Sanjay Mukherjee*

9. Zen Harmony with Earth and Sky : A Study of Sinha's "Harbour Lights" 86
   —*B.P. Sinha*

10. Daruwalla : His Language and Style 90
    —*Birendra Pandey*

11. The Nature of Conflict in Sri Aurobindo's *Perseus the Deliverer* 101
—Vinod Kumar Singh

12. The Spiritual Progress in the Poetry of T. Vasudeva Reddy 114
—T. Raghavan

13. Existentialism in the Poetry of O.P. Bhatnagar 123
—Kumari Vibha Agrawal

14. Womanhood Enmeshed in the Web of Tradition and Modernity : A Comparison between Balamani Amma's and Kamala Das's Ideas 130
—P.S. Radha

15. Quest for Self-Realisation in Nissim Ezekiel's Poetry 147
—M.K. Pandey

16. The Poetry of Maha Nand Sharma 154
—V.K. Arora

17. Towards a Rise of Consciousness : Humanism in Emerson and Sri Aurobindo (Man *vs.* Society) 159
—B.C. Dwivedy

18. Human Crisis and Superstition in 'Night of the Scorpion' 164
—Mrs. Qamar Talat

19. Orientalism in Nissim Ezekiel 168
—A.A. Khan

20. The First Milestone : A Critique of Sinha's *Harbour Lights* 173
—Asha Choubey

List of Contributors 182

1

East-West Encounter in Indian Poetry in English

—O.P. Bhatnagar

Indian poetry in English is a poetry of encounter. The encounter is not merely with language but with all the content of religion, culture, values, thoughts and attitudes which it unfolds as challenges to our sensibilities. It is not so much the British rule as the introduction of English language which unhinged our identity, confidence and conduct. That is why, while some noticed in the minutes of Macaulay a conspiracy to subvert Indian identity and culture, others regarded it as the precursor of Renaissance in India. The fall outs from this situation were contradictory and paradoxical. While anglicization made the educated people get too ready to disown their own culture and past and eulogize whatever was British the nationalistic spirit led to a revival of interest in our ancient heritage and culture. That India asserted itself through a foreign medium of expression is yet another paradox. As if India would have remained a slave country or would not have discovered itself but for English. In his book *Foundations of New India*, K.M. Pannikar goes to the extent of saying that but for English the Hindu community would have split into as many different units as there were languages in India after the pattern of Europe. Such instance of self-flagellation created other sets of paradoxes to be faced and resolved in future.

Whatever may have been the socio-political and cultural consequences of the introduction of English in India, it did create a situation which may broadly be described as one of east-west encounter. What exactly were the elements of this encounter and what did it imply in the creative field, specially poetry, alone forms our concern here. First of all the uses of English itself became an encounter. The immediate question was one of choosing a model in language use and creativity. The earliest Indian poets in English were greatly influenced by Byron, Shelley, Keats and Wordsworth and hence they chose to emulate them in spirit, form and expression. Note the tone, texture and syntax of Henry Derozio's The Harp of India.

Why hang'st thou lonely on your withered bough ?
Unstrung for ever, must thou there remain
The music was once great who hears it now ?
Why doth the breeze sign over thee in vam
Silence has bound thee with her fatal charm

Michael Madhusudan Dutt followed in the same vein as can be observed in the following lines from the *The Queen of Delhi's Dream :*

Methought there came a warrior-maid
With blood stained brow and sheathless blade
Dark was here hue, as darkest cloud,
And 'round her waist a hideous zone
Of hands with Charnel lightnings shone
And long the garland which she wove
Of heads all bath'd in streaming pore

Toru Dutt, Aru Dutt, Romesh Chander Dutt and Manmohan Ghose exhibited grea' love for the history and landscape of India and fine craftsmanship in the art of writing poetry matching English meters, the technical effects, the deft use of couplet in translation with long eight beat line with its trochees and anapests. A few lines from Toru Dutt's 'The Lotus' would give us an idea of what these poets were aiming were aiming to achieve and perform :

Love came to Flora asking for a flower
That would of flowers be undisputed queen
The lily and the rose, long, long had been
Rivals for that high honour. Bards of Power
Had sung their claim. The rose can never tower
Like the pale lily with her June mien

But is the lily lovelier? Thus between
Flower factions rang the strife in Psyche's bower.

Most of the poets came from the upper strata of society of whose associations with England and Europe and Christianity were quite close. They encountered the language situation by drawing models from British romantic poetry but they diffused the content by introducing themes from Indian history, myths and legends and thus paving away for possible union between east and west. The fact that they were writing in English created neither vacuum nor anxiety in them. The Indian history, heroes and culture were welded into the foreign medium without any conscious efforts.

Tagore poured forth the entire mystical vision of India and his richness of feelings of 'bhakti' into a foreign medium. But more important was his imagery drawn from the founts of Indian aesthetic, history, culture, rituals and festivals of the country. Such is the impress of Tagore's personality and force of emotions that the medium tends to loosen on its alienness and gathers a texture which cannot be missed for its being Indian. Look at the following lines from *Gitanjali* :

Thou hast made me endless, such is thy pleasure
This frail vessel thou emptiest again and again,
And fillest it ever with fresh life

Here, Tagore does not even have to introduce dialect or native words to make it look being used by an Indian in Indian contexts. Tagore's basic interest was content and not medium and as such he was able to overcome or reduce the gap between content and expression to his creative advantage, his voice, which he valued more than the wider reading public abroad.

Aurobindo was a still greater genius in this regard. He fused English with the rich spirit and store of India's ancient myths, conceptions of creation and evolution even at the risk of being alienated from the mainstream of the English reading public in the world, which setback has stuck to him even till this day. The vision, the voice, the gesture, the tone and the texture of Aurobindo's art is so firm and distinct that it cannot be separated by any morphological objective ideals in the criticism of his poetry. He used substantial vocabulary, metaphors and symbols drawn from the deepest layers of the ancient Indian culture and heritage not only to make poetry in English native but also to expand and extend upon its poetics. He introduced into the texture of English language hitherto certain inconscient areas of experience. Look at the magnificent handing of English in the opening of the epic *Savitri* :

It was the hour before the Gods awake.
Across the path of the divine Event
The huge foreboding mind of Night, alone
In her unlit temple of eternity,
Lay stretched immobile upon silence's marge
Almost one felt, opaque impenetrable
In the sombre symbol of her eyeless muse
The abysm of the unbodied Infinite,
A fathomless zero occupied the world.

A synthesis of a politician, a philosopher and a poet as he was he had a message of action for Indians in their struggle for independence and a direction for human progress towards supermanhood in his poetry. He was not only a master of blank verse but also a giant of English prosody. The great evocative power and sensuousness of Aurobindo remains unparalleled in Indian poetry in English, which can be marked in the following lines :

She, O'erborne
Ranting, with inarticulate murmurs lay,
Like a slim tree half seen through driving hail,
Her naked arms clasping his neck, her cheek
And golden throat averted, and wide trouble
In her large eyes bewildered with their bliss.
Amid her wind blown hair their faces met
With her sweet limbs all his feeling her breasts
Tumultuous up against his beating heart.
He kissed the glorious mouth of heaven's desire
So clung they as two shipwrecked in a surge

It may thus be noted that both for Tagore and Aurobindo English as language did not present any encounter. It in no way dislodged their sensibilities nor posed a threat to their identities. They were however more concerned with the content and bearings of the Indian identity, culture and heritage. They contended it by recreating the mores of our cultural heritage, vision and wisdom in the very language the colonizers had used to alienate the Indians from their roots. Their contribution therefore lies in decoding English of its British and Western connotations and coding it with Indian and Eastern denotations in the creative field. That is why the use of Indian landscape legends and history by the earlier poets did not change the texture of English as much as it did with Tagore and Aurobindo. The firmness of their faith and voice also spared them of any feigned nostalgia as felt by some of the later poets of the century.

Sarojini Naidu both extended and expanded the frontiers of Indian poetry in English. She too never suffered any pangs of alienation or cultural displacement in her encounter with English as a medium of creative and native expression. She gave up writing in modes, religious, spiritual or patriotic, and preferred to delve deep into experience and strike a personal note in poetry. She had no message to give except recreate the beauty, the aspects of love, the rhythm in movement and music surrounding her life. Her voice was not stifled either by her use of English or by her sojourns abroad. She could still sing like a free bird unfettered by any encounter of language or foreign culture telling upon her creativity. Look at the admirable way she could reproduce the atmosphere and lilt of folk-life and songs of India in English. Thus the palanquin bearers sang

> Lightly, O lightly, we bear her along,
> She always alike a flower in the wind of our song,
> She skims like a bird on the foam of a stream,
> She floats like a laugh from the lips of a dream,
> Gaily, O gaily we glide and we sing,
> We bear her along like a pearl on a string...

Or the Wandering Singers :

> Our lays are of cities whose luster is shed,
> The laughter and beauty of women long dead,

The sword of old battles, the crown of old kings,
And happy and simple and sorrowful things

Or the Coromandal Fishers :

Sweet is the shade of the coconut glade, and
The scent of the mango grove.
And sweet are the sands at the full O the moon with
The sound of the voices we love
But sweeter, O brothers the kiss of the spray and

It is not merely her eye and ear but also her heat which pours form into her lyrics and songs with such authenticity as to make the Glasgo Herald say that her poetry "Seems to prove that the best song knows nothing of East or West," and the Yorkshire Post acknowledge that "Mrs. Naidu has not only enriched our language but has enabled to grow into intimate relation with the spirit, the emotions, the mysticism and the glamour of the East." She was so versatile that she could write love and devotional songs with as much felicity as patriotic songs, dirges and elegies. It was so because she wrote with the confidence of an Indian without ever hesitating or doubting if she would be able to get herself across to others in a foreign language. In other words, she never got to be conscious of her use of English for the purposes of creative expression. Her clarity of vision made the medium transparent enough to be handled naturally and with ease. There was no attempt at any affectation or making towards modernity in her poetry.

Sarojini Naidu thus sums up the first phase of the movement of encountering English as the medium of expression in poetry. What started as the imitation of the British modes and models in Derozio ends up in projecting the Indian lore and spirit in a native way. The cultural contents of the language were contained by the pride, faith and conviction of the Indian heritage among the poets. English was used as a tool to embattle the vanity of the masters as a superior race and culture. And the battle was fought while the British were right here in India. All these poets wrote in English to mark their competence and not exhibit their slavery. All of them, specially Tagore and Aurobindo, presented a sense of the exclusiveness and self-sufficiency of Indian tradition. That is why the latter did not suffer from any cultural vacuum created by the encounter. They found their culture in no way inferior to that of the colonizer. On the objective analysis they pleaded for taking "from the West whatever is worthwhile." In The Renaissance in India, Aurobindo wrote about admitting, "Western science, reason, progressiveness, the essential modern ideas, but on our own way of life and assimilated to our spiritual aim and ideal." In fact, they explored as to how our ancient tradition could operate and function in the modern times.

But the rejection of the poetry written during the first phase culminating in the poetry of Aurobindo by P. Lal in his introduction to *Modern Indian Poetry in English* was short-sighted. He declared that "This kind so slushy verse is the most dangerous thing that infects our poetry today. It has spoilt a good deal of the Indo-Anglian past; it can without exaggeration spell ruin for the future. For an off-shoot of English poetry trying to establish roots in rocky ground, having a small and gradually dwindling public, such nebulosity in form and substance can be positively pernicious. Even the best Indo-Anglian poets writing now are not always entirely free from the clutches of soul-stuff. The temptation to slip into greasy, weakspined and purple-adjective "spiritual" poetry always exists, it exists especially in the case of poet who has failed to realize that the art of poetry is an art exacting and painstaking as the carving of an original design in ivory."

But in the process what did the P. Lal manifesto produce in P. Lal's poetry itself thinness of poetry and poetic content for simplicity and unaffectedness without effect. Look at the following extract from the 'Parrot's Death'

If it were less beautiful
And my eyes did not catch beauty,
If in the morning
My eyes did not catch beauty,
I would have peace

Or extracts from his love poems :

White rose in black hair

Is for me I suppose
Or
My love is no less bright
Than these bright birds today
In the diffuse delight
Of sun and wind at play

Or the lines from 'The Morning Moon at Mussoorie'.

Where up beyond the deodars
Clouds scud in iambic rhyme
And the moon keeps time, keeps time

These extracts are not only adolescent but also betray the shallowness of experience and poverty of reflection. But his transcreations have more poetry in them than his original poetry. The following lines from Rigvedic Songs on Agni would amply justify the contrast.

He (Agni) shines like a white horse among men,
Like a golden chariot made ready for battle,
His passion like an army marches, or
Like an archer's arrow shooting to its point.

To my mind, all these pronouncements were made for fear of "a small and gradually dwindling public", in the post-independence era. Such a nebulous criterion led to the disembodiment and dismemberment of the organicity of both identity and vision of Indian poetry in English. The poets writing in the early post-independence era ran after catching a wider reading public abroad working-up exile, alienation, identity crisis on the one hand and satire, parody and mockery of Indian character, style and values on the other, thus turning O. Mannoni's table of effects of colonization for adulation to disillusionment, rebellion and rejection the other way round. These poets cannot be called as revivalists. They had the just kind of pride, respect and love for their ancient heritage. They were aware of certain socio-cultural shortcomings of their own country as well as the achievements of the West and called for profit from the encounter in their other writings. But the content of their poetry reflecting the creative engagement of their imagination to be occupied with the rebuilding of the image of India in terms of its ancient heroes, history, ideals and philosophy to say with Chinua Achebe that our "past — with all its imperfections — was not one long night of savagery from which the first European acting on God's behalf delivered them."

With the dawn of independence the Indian poetic sensibility undergoes a sea change. In its attempt to be modern it gives up the organicity of its comprehensive vision and becomes personal and individualistic. Suddenly, the poets become conscious of the controversy over the necessity of writing in English. The question of language becomes personal history. The encounter generates some self-searching and new insights into cultural identity. Sometimes it creates a sense of mockery and comic exposure of the absurdity created by the cross cultural and linguistic conflicts. While some become bold to analyse and debunk the attitudes and conduct of Indians others play to western gallery and amusement and parade the nakedness and wretchedness of India. Yet others go long distances in the West to affect nostalgia or self-discovery. Some take to hybridization of imagery, turn metropolitan and take to the very values, modes and manners which the Westerners themselves are abandoning or fleeing from. Others exhibit colonial dependent behaviour. That is why the purist application to English grew malignant in the post-independence era. The people not only compared the kind of English Indians were writing with that of the British but also questioned to propriety of Indians writing poetry in English at all. The manner of saying gathered credence than the thing said, thus making room for concrete images and imagery than vision forming or informing a poem. The western influence or manner in poetry was more intense now than ever before. It was so because of the increasing and wider expousure of the Indians to the other English speaking regions beyond England. The West therefore becomes more charming and worth cultivating its style and grace of expression so as to become native with it. Yet the perceptive ones tried to breathe of sanity and synthesis of values, modes, manner and matter, past and present and spontaneity and restraint.

In post-independence era, English as language became a fresh reality to contain and react to. Kamala Das justifies the use of English in her own way :

> Don't write in English, they said
> English is not your mother-tongue. Why not leave
> Me alone, critics, friends, visiting cousins.
> Everyone of you? Why not let me speak in
> Any language I like? The language I speak
> Becomes mine, its distortions, its queerness
> All mine, mine along

But R. Parthasarathy reacts to the situation in a different way. He brings out the pathos of it in the following way :

> My tongue in English chains
> I return, after a generation, to you
> I am at the end
>
> Of my dravidic tether.
> Hunger for you unassuaged

Reflecting on the situation A.K. Ramanujan presents the nature of relationships between English and native language for creative purpose in his own case as follows :

> "English and my disciplines (linguistics, anthropology) give me my 'outer' forms linguistic, metrical, logical and other such ways if shaping experience, and my personal and professional preoccupations with Kannada, Tamil give me my substance, my 'inner' forms, images and symbols."

Given these musings Nissim Ezekiel found enough room to mock at the Indian use of English in one of his poems. Goodbye Party for Miss Pushpa T.S. :

> Friends
> Our dear sister
> Is departing for foreign
> In two three days,
> And
> We are meeting today
> To wish her bon voyage

You are all knowing friends.
What sweetness is in Miss Pushpa
I don't mean only external sweetness
But internal sweetness
Miss Pushpa is smiling and smiling
Even for no reason
But simply because she is feeling.

Freedom made it easy for Indians to go west and make it their home for convenience or comfort. While thus encountering west some felt alienated, or as if in exile, and others look to nostalgia about their past life in India. An extract from R. Parthasarathy's 'Rough Passage' reads as follows :

He had spent his youth whoring
After English gods
There is something to be said for exile
You learn roots are deep.
That language is a tree, loses colour
Under another sky.

The entire poetry of A.K. Ramanujan is recollection of his life and childhood in India. While in the west the memories of Indian past return with a greater force and intensity and crystallize in a tone and imagery which stands out different from the Indian look at some of the lines from his poem 'Small Scale Reflections on a Great House' :

Unread library books
Usually mature in two weeks
And begin to lay a row
Of little eggs in the ledgers
For lines, as silverfish
In the old man's office room
Breed dynasties among long legal words
Of Victorian parchment

Whatever may be said for and against such a product the Indian poet-does show a split — linguistic personality, which, if it helps him overcome anomie and deracination it also tells on his capacity to evoke immediate aesthetic response with his synthetic imagery.

But unlike A.K. Ramanujan, Dom Moraes and many others, Nissim Ezekiel struggles with himself to say :

I have made my commitments now.
This is one to stay where I am,
As others choose to give themselves
In some remote and backward place
My backward place is where I am

It is for this reason that he exhibits the best possible synthesis of the east and west. One could attribute yet another reason for his proportion and balance between the two extremes. His Jewish origin gives him the necessary distance from both to be objective. He looks at the traditional attitudes towards love and religion from a modern point of view and pleads for an existential plunge and experience of life. May be such an enterprise may end in disgust but it is worthwhile undergoing for the wisdom of it :

When finally we reached the place
We hardly knew why we were there
The trip had darkened every face.
Our deeds were neither great nor rare.
Home is where we have to gather grace.

A certain frankness of attitude towards sex and love is the direct outcome of the east-west encounter. Look at 'The Looking Glass of Kamala Das' :

Getting a man to love you is easy
Only be honest about your wants as
Women. Stand nude before the glass with him
So that he sees himself the stronger one
And believe it so, and you so much more
Softer, younger, lovelier. Admit your
Admiration. Notice the perfection
Of his limbs, his eyes reddening under
The shower, the shy walk across the bathroom floor.
Dropping towels, and the jerky way he
Urinates. All the fond details that make
Him male and your only man. Gift him ali,
Gift him what makes you woman, the scent of
Long hair, the musk of sweet between the breasts.

> The warm shock of menstrual blood, and all your
> Endless female hungers.

For a refreshing change the encounter also provided enough room and freedom to make light even of one's own religion and gods. In 'Heart of Ruin' this is how Arun Kolatkar refers to Maruti :

> The roof comes down on Maruti's head
> Nobody seems to mind
> Least of all Maruti himself.

In 'The Door' this is what he observes :

> The door would have walked out
> Long long ago
> If it weren't for
> That pair of shorts
> Left to dry upon its shoulders.

Gods are revealed in 'A Low Temple' as follows :

> You lend a matchbox to the priest
> One by one the Gods come to light.

If, by such a kind of humour, sarcasm and irony, English as a third medium, did work to the calculated designs of the Colonizer in dismantling some part of one's filiations to one's culture, race and ethnicity, it also facilitated the anglicized writer maintaining his own distance on the medium by destroying it through new structures and linguistic turns, flavoured by the native sensibilities, to such an extent as to become a new medium of expression of the Colonizer himself.

With Jayanta Mahapartra Indian poetry in English has come full circle. There is no encounter with any of the east-west encounter stereotypes. If language is "non-native" it is suffused with native spirit and emotions. The spirit is of landscape and emotions that pride in the heritage of the land making the medium malleable enough to be native and act native. It is this nativization of English which remains the greatest contribution of Jayanta Mahapatra to Indian poetry in English. This achievement has followed his open eyed identification not only with the landscape but also with its traditions, myths and legends forming a whole.

One has only to experience his emotional use of the elemental in Oriya landscape rains, both as symbol and reality in all ramifications. Feel the following examples :

> All night I have waited for the rain to end,
> The forbidden memories ringing, compelling
> Footfalls among the ruins, the day's last sun-smoking
> In unending fields soaked in innocence
>
> (*Four Rain Poems*)

Or

> I see
> It play over people, piled up to their silences
> It creates an impression of vastness
> It quietly opens a door. (*A Rain*)

Or

> Rain that falls silently in July sky
> Catching in your trembling skin pearls of fire
> Who can bear the thought
> Of his woman going out with someone else
> Rain falling on with frightened eyes
> Clay that bites the one
> Who gave it life (*The Rain Falling*)

The temple of Lord Jagannath at Puri is not only suffused with the halos of myth but also serves as a symbols of 'nirvana' which makes endless streams of pilgrims line up the temple in devotion :

> Later
> As the shrine's skeins of light
> Slowly close their eyes,
> Something reaching into them
> From the place they learn
> The lame lamp pcst
> To the huge temple door,
> The sacred beads in their hands

Gaping
At the human ground (*The Temple Road, Puri*)

In an emotional upsurge of feelings for the vanquished pride that was cuttack with its proud Barabati Fort the poet records :

Now I stand among the ruins
Waiting for the cry of a night bird
From the river's far side
To drift through my weariness
Listening to the voices of my friends
Who have become the friends of others
Writing poems, abject and anxious
In rooms which reek of old folk,
Of their sloth and arthritis and neglect
Like state cupboards which are going black
With the smells of her rancid fat of the past.
(*Relationship*)

In his effort to identify himself with the "Living Oriya past" Jayanta Mahapatra has made his poetry not only a medium of reviving memory but a living presence. In him Indian poetry in English has become palpable.

With the period of incubation over, Indian poetry in English has flourished as a liberalized art. Its quality can be measured by the publication of over a hundred volumes per year pouring in from people from all walks of life and genders. The thrust of women poets is so strong that one is tempted to call it feminine with an aesthetic of its own. The new poetry is free from the anxiety of exile, alienation, crisis of identity pickle, justification of writing in English or writing poetry in English at all.

2

Daruwalla : A Poet in Search of Identity

—*R.A. Singh*

Keki N. Daruwalla is one of the most talented living poets who made their presence felt in early sixties. He is a growing poet in Indian English poetry. His collection of poems include : *Under Orion* (1970), *Apparition in April* (1971), *Crossing of Rivers* (1976), *Winter Poems* (1980), *The Keeper of the Dead* (1982) and *Landscapes* (1987). In recognition of his talent, he was awarded the Sahitya Akademi award for *The Keeper of the Dead.* Though his poetic output is meagre, it is of enduring quality. He has written poems on various themes such as growing corruption in public life, communal craze, black marketing and profiteering, religious orthodoxy, lovelessness, rootlessness and so on and so forth. Like other modern poets he, too, has drifted apart from the older poets so far subject matters and their treatment is concerned. Daruwalla writes in free verse, though there is rhyming scheme, it is not always coherent. The way of presentation is mostly narrative. Thus, there is a complete departure from the established tradition. With his man-alone in a hostile world attitude, Daruwalla has moved poetry into new dimensions.

The portrait of man, in much of recent Indian English poetry, is that of the alienated individual, rootless and helpless, psychologically restrained and passive, cautiously retreating to the inner world after his each faint encounter with the reality. Here the case is a more or less severe form of psychic numbing. The loss of identity that marks the lives of men and women in the present commercial civilization is conveyed in the poetry of many Indian poets writing in English.

Modern man is bound to suffer from loneliness and pangs of separation as every day he grows a stranger to himself as well as to his milieu. The rapport between man and man is missing because of the sense of alienation gripping us today. Amidst crowd and vast population, a sensitive writer finds himself utterly lonely. Darkness prevails everywhere and a modern man's life is marked by dark and deep fears. Daruwalla finds :

> The tree is now all bark and bough
> Leafless twigs scratch
> against the glass
> like skeletal children
> Scribbling on a slate,
> Chalk-fingered.

(*Winter Poems*)

The phrase 'Chalk fingered' suggests lack of vitality and life, it is a symbol of deprivation. The modern man is drained of vitality and has become rather introvert. He has parted with the passions as do the flakes of dandruff :

> The expressions ripped away
> like torn wings
> its passions flaking off
> like dandruff...

(*Winter Poems*)

Daruwalla beautifully expresses man's helplessness. He tells that the ghosts of man's glorious past keep on hunting. Man is terror-struck :

> I heard the thick waters of your dreams
> Lap the shores of your night :
> behind your rhinestone eyes
> flickered a flame of terror.

(*Winter Poems*)

In spite of all his efforts to forget his past to mould him as the present demands, man sometimes fails to cope himself with the changed situation. He remains awestruck and dumb founded. The shocks remain fixed in his psyche till his death :

but you tucked the dream
within the sleave of your body.
It lies coffined in your psyche...
(*Winter Poems*)

Daruwalla presents a fine sketch of man. His body has a tumorous growth, his skin is 'raffia', his hair growing very thin and his case is now of 'charred ribs'. He is completely helpless, even the voice sticks in his throat and he finds horrifying darkness looming around him :

...as if a gland
in the tree's groin
had turned tumorous
but the nest is lined
with cotton seed
and raffia
overhead the mother kite
Keen
circling anxiously....
(*Winter Poems*)

Daruwalla vivifies the feelings of the man at the threshold when he is grasped by a queer feeling and suffers from a sense of alienation in this world. The poet gives vent to his feelings in the following lines :

We have come of age
those who grew with us
have started dying.
(*Winter Poems*)

The poet says that the man is now cut off from worldly love and affection and he is living a painful life. He is standing at the cross-roads searching his identity :

Something to make the cross roads less cruel,
Something to hold back
the seething tide of memory...
(*Winter Poems*)

Here the man wishes to be possessed of a sense of detachment, if not spontaneously forced one. The poet observes :

and this grudging acceptance
from the heart we need like
gluttinous mick from the
lanced poppy — that nothing but nothing
belongs to us.
let's adjust to shifts of light
and shifts of shadow.

(*Winter Poems*)

The man's feelings confirm the nothingness of life. Like other great poets and playwrights, Daruwalla too admits the world to be illusive with one difference. He preaches the sermon of detachment. This shows the great influence of *The Bhagwad Geeta* on him.

The poet is worried to find the tap of his imagination drying up very rapidly :

and the forest of imagination
like the forest of the earth,
turning to deserts;
and the skies closing in
like claustrophic mist.

The agony and anguish of loneliness of these lines is comparable to the loneliness of the following lines by Robert Frost :

One aged man-can't keep a house
A farm, a countryside, or if he can,
It's thus he does it of a winter night.

Presenting the modern man torn between doubt and belief, lust and guilt, and artificial and natural the poet bitterly remarks :

While we oscillate between the fires of lust and
guilt seeking our refuge in those air tight,
air conditioned pharmacies of the heart
where the antidotes to the guilt are being prepared.

(*The Keeper of the Dead*)

Revealing the inner chagrin and agony of the modern man at his own indiscretion. The poet satirically enumerates :

...We bleed on for half a life time and find
the effort

wasted. Negative parasites, despising what
we feed on.

. . .

(*The Keeper of the Dead*)

The poet digs at the mechanical and artificial life of the modern men, suffering from lovelessness and tastelessness. Juxtaposing the attributes of the present and the past, the poet laughs at the misery of the present :

...I quiver with flab and fatigue, bad reflexes and
bad faith
yet across my jaded appetites a longing reaches out.

(*The Keeper of the Dead*)

Struggling hard to find out his destination the man becomes a 'nowhereman' and accepts the hard realities of life and in this way comes to the solitudes :

The solitudes are beneath us now,
of ice, of desert, of corrugated cloud.

(*The Landscapes*)

REFERENCES

1. Daruwalla Keki N., *The Winter Poems* (1980), Allied Pub., Bombay.
2. ——, *The Keeper of the Dead* (1982), Oxford University Press, Delhi.
3. ——, *The Landscapes* (1987), Oxford University Press, Delhi.
4. ——, *Two Decades of Indian Poetry* (1980), Vikas Pub., New Delhi.
5. R.A. Singh, *Keki N. Daruwalla : Assessment As Poet*, Prakash Book Depot, Bareilly, 1991.
6. ——, *Keki N. Daruwalla : The Keeper of the Dead (A Critical Study)*, Prakash Book Depot, Bareilly, 1992.

3

A Ramayana for Women : K.R. Srinivasa Iyengar's *Sitayana*

—*P. Raja*

Indian Writing in English that began with the publication of Cavelly Venkata Boriah's *The Account of the Jains* in the year 1808 has established itself as one among the major literatures of the world. A dip into the voluminous information guide titled *Indian Literature in English, 1827-1979*[1] vindicates this claim. Yet in the history of this nearly 200 years old literature we come across only one epic poem *Savitri*, authored by a yogi, philosopher and poet — Sri Aurobindo.

Readers and critics of Indian Writing in English have always wondered what new epic would come in the wake of Sri Aurobindo's *Savitri*. "What? An epic! And that too in verse!" Even the voluminous writers are said to have remarked so and shrugged their shoulders. Hence the hope of reading another epic was slowly vanishing. But one fine morning Samata Books, Madras surprised the literary world by releasing an epic in verse — *Sitayana* written by Dr. K.R. Srinivasa Iyengar, critic, literary historian and a poet in his own right. Like his master Sri Aurobindo, he has named his epic after its heroine. Sri Aurobindo's epic with all its mystical turns and abstruse language is extremely hard to decipher, since the poet himself once declared that he had not written *Savitri* for anybody but himself. But Iyengar's *Sitayana* is every man's or rather every woman's cup of tea.

At the suggestion of a friend, Dr. Iyengar wished to try

his hand at an English verse rendering of an abridged *Ramayana*. But the spate of one-volume versions of *Ramayana* by eminent writers like Rajaji, R.K. Narayan, Kamala Subramaniam, P. Lal and others discouraged him. "It then occurred to me," writes Iyengar in the introduction to his epic, "perhaps, I might attempt on my own a fresh recital of the *Ramayana* story but slanted as *Sitayana, Sitayana Caritam Mahat*. Sita's saga sublime... with something like a reckless presumption I wished to retell the *Ramayana as Sitayana* in about a fourth of a length of Valmiki's massive and magnificent poetic recordation" (pp : viii-ix).

Borrowed heavily from Valmiki's *Ramayana*, occasionally from Kamban's Tamil epic *Ramayanam* and more occasionally from Tulsi Das's *Rama Charita Manasa*, Dr. Iyengar's *Sitayana* : *Epic of the Earth-Born* retells the same old story of Rama, for what is Sita without her Rama. Perhaps Iyengar's question is what is Rama without her Sita. Hence *Sitayana* is the story of Sita, and of her vicissitudes of her human relationship with Rama.

Sitayana was written over a period of about three years. A remarkable achievement indeed for it is on record that Virgil devoted approximately ten years to his *Aeneid*, Dante sixteen intermittently and six wholly to his *Divina Commedia*, Milton at least eight to *Paradise Lost* and Goethe spread the writing of his *Faust*, with long intervals, over nearly fifty years of crowded life. And *Savitri, a Legend and a Symbol* over which Sri Aurobindo had worked for almost his life time.[2] Dr. Iyengar's epic spans Sita's life from her birth in a furrow to her later return to the bowels of the earth. Between the beginning and the end moves the story of her childhood and her girlhood, her marriage to Rama, their life as exiles in Dandaka for 13 years, their year long separation and reunion, their coronation at Ayodhya, her second sundering from Rama, her crown of motherhood and her self transcendence. Divided into seven books, each of eleven cantos and written in the unrhymed quatrain measure *Sitayana's* success lies in the fitful recordation of the aches, exultations, soul-searching of the blemish less Earth-born.

If Sita, the beauty of innocence, freshness, self-sufficiency, the perfect fusion of all perfections, the exemplum feminine is not a good subject matter for an epic, where is subject matter to be found?

Iyengar's purpose in writing this epic is made clear in the first quatrain of the 'Prologue' itself :

> Of womanhood I write, of the travail
> and glory of motherhood;
> of Prakriti and her infinite modes
> and unceasing variety (p. xix).

Through Ahalya, Iyengar brings to limelight the status of women in the present day society. When a cyclonic wind drives Sita and Urmila to the hermitage of Ahalya, the frail and flawed woman comes out of the clinging clouds of viperous memory. Shaken by spasms anew, Ahalya foresees the fate of women :

> Past the long millenniums of chequered
> terrestrial history,
> I see the degraded, demoralized
> toy, sport, game, fun, footstool, slave :
>
> a consumerist piece of merchandise
> to be bought, got, bartered, sold,
> used, misused, abused, or left long unused
> and callously cast away. (p. 107)

The protest of women against male supremacy rings throughout this epic. The outbursts of Ahalya :

> I see things — how shall I now describe them? —
> I see such horrendous things,
> sepulchral sequences and denouements
> that defy understanding.
>
> I see Man stopping low enough to shame
> the Asura and the Beast;
> I see Woman unfeminised, flaunting
> her crass unwomanliness.
>
> Not the worst yet : I see the devil-dance

of the seven deadly sins;
I see women staled, enslaved; and female
children cast out unwanted.

I see widows on the funeral pyres
of their late partners in life,
and I see child widows of cherubim
innocence branded with sin!

None is spared, alas, only degraded
with abominations done
to their persons and psyches; and I see
bride-burnings and dowry-deaths!

Why have I returned to life to view these
precipitous descents from
Woman as Shakti and Grace to Woman
as object and possession! (p. 106)

The harpings of Tara, Vali's wife, on male and female relationship :

what governs male-female relationships
is a shifting, elastic,
evolutionary ethic, changing
with the changing times and mores.

The purity of mind and heart and soul
is the quintessential mark,
for the body's self-protection from taints
fails sometimes, or isn't enough.

Because a lecher is unscrupulous —
albeit a king or a god! —
and seizes or forces a hapless one,
shall we consign her to hell? (p. 526)

Trijata's musings on womanhood :

Woman is often admired and cherished,
installed on a pedestal

as Shakti, Sundari, Grihalakshmi,
or Mahasaraswati;
but her sacredness is expendable,
she is property for sale,
a pretty piece for gambling at the board,
a ready cake to swallow!

'Puissance' her name, and 'puissance' her birthright;
were it not for her puissance
Woman couldn't be the Mother of the race,
the fosterer of mankind.

Yet by force of custom she's diminished
being caged in gold, curtained
by silk that's stronger than steel, and branded
as the temptress fair or foul. (pp. 458-459)

and Lopamudra's digs and taunts at the whole encyclopedia of do's and don'ts for the woman, contrasted with the flagrantly opposite guidebook for the domineering male :

'Don't speak too loud!' the hapless girl is told;
'Don't walk too fast, don't come out
of the cribbed security of the home;
in or out obey the male!'

O engage, if you will, in childhood games,
play the nurse with pretty dolls,
or act the sage mother with other girls,
or chatter with your parrots!

Marry at the proper time, bear children;
and let the sons and daughters
grow and evolve like different species—
and don't presume to question!

And look, Sita, how from his very birth
the boy has a privileged
upbringing; he's the superior sex,
the ruler, fighter, killer.

His childhood toys are soldiers, his boyhood
occupation is playing
with bows, arrows, axes, maces, tridents
and dreaming of streams of blood.

Alas, alas, what a mess humankind
has made the gifts of the Grace
vouchsafed equally to men and women
by the Mother of us all! (pp. 216-217)

are a few samples of the bombshells that make a Hiroshima of male chauvinism. Dr. Iyengar's powerful language whizzes like bullets freed from a high-powered machine gun, and even a Rama (byword for an ideal husband) can't escape unscathed.

"My ideal of a wife is Sita," wrote Mahatma Gandhi, "and of a husband Rama. But Sita was no slave to Rama."[3] To Sita, separation from Rama would be more horrible than the dangers in the forest. And so she says in the style of Omar Khayyam :

With you, Rama, by my side, Dandaka
were paradise enough... (p. 139)

for she is sure that her father Janaka chose a man as her husband and "not a woman in man's image" (p. 140). Is Iyengar hinting at the poor parents marrying off their daughters to old and impotent men?

Devotion to one's husband doesn't mean that one should remain blind to all his thoughtless actions. Iyengar depicts Sita as a good counsellor too. When Rama promises the Rishis inside Dandaka that he would rid them of the Rakshasa menace, she reminds him of Dharma's imperatives. It is no wonder that the women in her feels such repugnance to all forms of cruelty :

I grant I'm a woman, but Janaka's
daughter too, and Rama's wife :
how may I refrain from speech or counsel
when Dharma beats a retreat? (p. 193)

In spite of her duty-bound love for Rama, Sita does not behave like a slave. On one occasion, Rama unbalanced by the fast-tongued ogress — Rumour — arraigns Sita thus :

When you had perforce to live in his place,
Ravana couldn't have left you
undefiled, since you are so beautiful
and hence so desirable.

All the glory of pristine womanhood,
all the grace of purity,
perfection, all the fire of the true wife,
all have taken leave of you. (p. 490)

It is the best example of how the best of men at the best of times could be seized with idiocy. Sita rises like a fury. She finds apt words to express herself

Our happy years together are nothing,
Your green eye is everything! (p. 492)

Finally she curses her husband who has succumbed to the green-eyed monster :

...as the yokel that cast out a pearl
you'll now live in history. (p. 492)

But she does so only before her fire-baptism takes place. Yet when she is exiled again, she tells Lakshmana like a typical Indian woman :

For a woman, her husband is her god,
friend, comrade and counselor;
I'll therefore do what pleases my Lord,
aye, give up all joy of life? (p. 578)

The words come from the depth of her heart and touch our heartstrings, and we are remembered of Lopamudra's words :

The lunatic division of labour—
Woman for the home, and Man
for the battlefield! — has driven a wedge
and splintered humanity. (p. 217)

Sumitra, Lakshmana's mother, consoles the bereaved Sita thus : "Alas! Sufferance is woman's name!" and thereby summarises this epic in a single line. *Sitayana* contains some striking insights into the nature of male-female relationship and its implications in a male-dominated world. Listen to the lament of Mandodari :

> Woman's love — a mother's, wife's or sister's
> a daughter's, any woman's —
> by its own law fosters and sustains life,
> but the Male always assails
>
> With its pride, ambition, self-righteousness,
> and the woman pays, hapless
> Mankind pays, the entire commonwealth pays;
> but woman pays most of all. (p. 498)

Sita too musing bitterly on the knight-errants of lust whimpers thus :

> ...Women were but commodities, trophies
> or pieces of property.
>
> Woman was cheap — the Mother of the race
> was nothing, worse than nothing;
> Sisters, daughters — weren't they expendable?
> Sufferance was woman's name! (p. 546)

And again, in a to be or not to be scene, she philosophises on the evils of war and lechery :

> Oh, war, war, oh lechery, lechery!
> the twin debasing hobbies
> of the male that deaden and degrade him
> and make him the Asura! (p. 217)

and thereby makes a dig at the domineering male. Any man, worthy the name, will wince at the heated words of Lopamudra :

> But where shall we find strong enough language
> to castigate the follies
> and crimes, the jealousies and revenges,
> of the mindless human male? (p. 217)

A wife addressing her husband by his name is not anywhere in our Indian culture, be it Dravidian or Aryan. But the author allows his characters Sita, Urmila and Srutakirti to call their respective husbands by their names. Sita, of course, can't but call the name of Lord, when she is carried away by Ravana, and has to seek help. But on all other occasions the word 'Aryaputra' is forgotten, though Sita during the scene of her rejection by Rama (p. 491) utters "the word as of old" that is rich with infinite suggestion. Leave alone the youthful Sita and her sisters. Kaikeyi too, tempted by the hunchbacked old dame Manthara, rises like an incited cobra and hisses :

> Let him come, the doddering deceitful
> King : I'll sulk, I'll rave, I'll rage. (p. 124)

Since many quatrains are devoted to highlight the sufferings of women and the domination of men, it may not be taken for granted that Iyengar wishes to set women against men. He takes extra care to portray wife-hood. When Rama is exiled and likes Sita to be with her in-laws she delivers a speech tipped with fire. The following quatrain speaks of her mind about a true wife :

> For a wife, there's neither father, mother,
> son, friend, but her Lord alone :
> She shares his life as much in foul weather
> as in fair, and all the time. (p. 139)

Sita smiles through the rainbow of her tears. There lies the greatness of Sita, the ideal women.

Since the epic tells the saddest tale of Sita, there is no dearth of sweet dramatic poetry here. Be it the description of war or the physical beauty of women, be it the venom tipped speeches of the angry women on the arrogant male or the lament of Mandodhari, be it the incident of the Asura crow or the story of Hiranyakasipu, Iyengar is at his best.

Dr. Iyengar, no doubt, advocates woman's equality and he puts this point in a very subtle manner in the 'Prologue' itself. This epic is every woman's delight, especially to the members of Women's Liberation Movement; a whip for all "male-chauvinist pigs" and an enthralling work for lovers of Indian Writing in English. The contemporaneity of its appeal makes the long journey from 'Mithila' to 'Ashrama' an enjoyable one. It is a memorable experience to read *Sitayana* both for the ideas expressed and for the manner in which these ideas are marshalled with impeccable logic.

NOTES AND REFERENCES

All page references within the text are to the 1987 edition of *Sitayana* published by Samata Books, Madras.

1. Singh, Amritjit. Verma, Rajiva & Joshi, Irene M. (eds.), *Indian Literature in English, 1827-1979* (American literature, English literature and World literatures in English information guide series : V. 36) U.S.A. : Gale Research Company, 1981.
2. Sethna, K.D., *Sri Aurobindo : The Poet.* Pondicherry : Sri Aurobindo International Centre of Education, 1999, p. 136.
3. *Young India*, Oct. 21, 1926.

4

A.K. Ramanujan's "Two Days" : A Stylistic Study

—*G.D. Barche*

A.K. Ramanujan, with three volumes of verse, viz., *The Striders* (1966), *Relations* (1971), and *Selected Poems* (1976), has occupied a prominent place among the eminent Indian Poets in English. His use of English has been measured and masterly. He has coined new images to shape his freshly felt experiences about the truths of life. Here a short poem is taken up to examine his poetic prudence and potential. The poem is as follows :

Two Days

Yesterday, I met
no one :
It was wet
and vain :
a mouthful
of breath
on tomorrow's windowpane.

And today too was vain.
But I met
Someone
who gave it
pretensions to a pattern :
a maplike waterstain
Steaming upon a stone.[1]

This poem projects the wheel of life and time moving on from one day (yesterday) to another day (tomorrow) which in turn becomes (today) and which further glides down to (yesterday). This can be shown as follows :

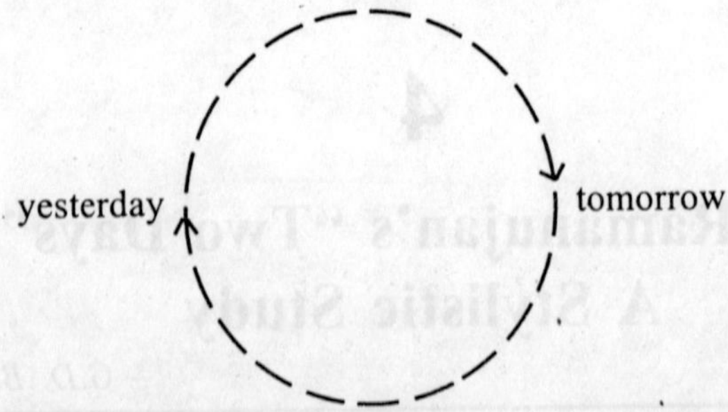

So apparently there appears to be three days, *viz.*, yesterday, today-tomorrow. But actually the process is confined to today and yesterday. That is, 'tomorrow' which is imaginatively visualized glides down to the actual 'today' and then this 'today' creeps into 'yesterday' which is imaginatively re-visualised. So really speaking, there aren't even two days but only one. It is because 'tomorrow' is nothing but a bunch of imaginatively visualized facts, while 'yesterday' is that of the actualized facts being imaginatively revisualised, and it is only 'today' that has the actual process of undergoing experiences. And hence, the title of the poem is significant. That is, in the spelling form it is 'Two Days', but as an instance of homophone when pronounced and transcribed it will be /tu deiz/ and can be taken as 'to Days' like "To Daffodils" by Herrick or 'todays', the plural form.

Now there is a man, the protagonist, who is caught in the wheel of life and time. He meets his friend at the close of 'today' and tells him that yesterday he met no one and that 'it was wet and vain' like 'a mouthful of breath on tomorrow's Windowpane'. Similarly, today too was vain. But today he met 'someone' who give it (wetness and vainness) pretensions (with) a pattern which was like 'a map of waterstain' that is left 'upon a stone' after water's evaporation. This can again be shown as under :

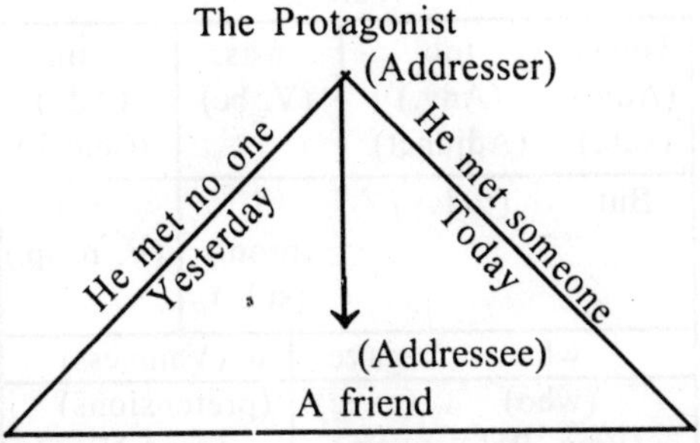

'it was wet and vain'
like
'a mouthful of breath
on tomorrow's windowpane.'

'(It) too was vain.' But 'someone' gave vainness 'Pretensions' with a pattern that appeared like a map of waterstain upon a stone.

Thus, the poem appears to present two sets of experiences of one day (yesterday) and the other day (today). But it is not the reality but illusion. The poet has tried to convey the truth that the distinctions such as yesterday-tomorrow-today are futile and that all worldly experiences begin in warmth and meaning, but end in emptiness, and nothingness. Then there are some people who try to attribute some patterned meaning to the nothingness and futility of life experiences, but then such attempts are equally futile.

Now let us see how the poet has expressed such a complex and touch truth of life through this outwardly so small and a simple poem. First let us rewrite the poem with some modifications as follows :

Two Days

	Part — 1			
(str. 1)	Yesterday (Adv.) (Adjunct)	I (Pron.) (Sub.)	met (Vrecip.)	no one (Pron. Neg.) (obj.)
(sub. str. 1)	it (Yesterday) (Pron.) (sub.)	was (vbe)	wet and vain *(Adj.) (Conj.) (Adj.)* (compl.)	
(sub. str. 2)	*a mouthful of breath* (NP)		*on tomorrow's windowpane* (Prep. Phr.)	

	(Part — 2)				
(str. 1)	Today (Adv.) (sub.)	too (Adv.) (Adjunct)	was (V. be)	vain (Adj.) (Compl.)	
(str. 2)	But	(today)	I (pron.) (sub.)	met (V. recip.)	someone (Pron. indef.) (obj.)
(sub. str. 1)	who	gave	it (Vainness)		pretensions
(a)	(who)	(gave)	(pretensions)		a pattern
(b)	(Pron. Rel.) (sub.)	(Vt.)	(Pro.) N (IO)		(N) (DO)
(sub. str. 3)	*a map like waterstain* (NP)		*Steaming* (PP)		*upon a stone* (Prep. Phr.)

Abbreviations : Str = structure, sub-str = sub = structure, sub = subject, obj = object, compl = complement, Adj = adjective, N = Noun, Pron = Pronoun, Adv = adverb, NP = Noun Phrase, Prep. Phr. = Prepositional Phrase, PP = Present participle.

Note : Words in the brackets are provided by me.

A close view of this presentation makes us see the use of Parallelistic Patterns having an element of identity and contrast at the levels of words, structures and sounds. First, it can be seen in the use of words such as : 'Wet and Vain'. Here the element of identity is seen in its structure as 'Adj and Adj', and then in its phonological congruence/wet n vein/. The contrast lies in the fact that 'wet' occurs with concrete nouns, *e.g.*, *wet* stone, while 'vain' with abstract ones, *e.g.*, *vain* attempt. Secondly, 'wet' broadly symbolizes positive aspect, *e.g.*, wetness of feelings or 'it is the wetness that gives sustenance to all, while 'vain' goes with negative aspect as it means futile, useless, meaningless. Then the conjunction 'and' brings the parallel bond between the two. That is, though the two are surfacially different and even opposite, but at bottom both are one in the sense that something may appear abstract, warm and meaningful or concrete cold and destructive, ultimately both end into emptiness and nothingness.

Further Parallelism can be seen at the sentence level. The

poem consists of three sentences : 1ii : 1 + 1ii forwarding and fusing two sets of experiences, Sub-str. 1 in Part one, and str. 1 in Part two are identical except the variant elements like 'yesterday' and 'today.' Further, the word 'wet' is deleted in str. 1 of part two. This way the poet has tried to show the truth that apparently the life is seen being governed by 'yesterday' and 'today'; and 'wet and vain', *i.e.*, meaningfulness and meaninglessness, but then the time is an endless flow and the terms such as 'yesterday' and 'today' and 'wet and vain' appear real for practical purposes but redundant in infinite flow of life and time and at the end vainness alone stands out.

The str. 1 in part one and str. 2 in part two are parallel and identical except the variant elements like 'no one' and 'someone' and the deletion of 'today' for economy. Further 'someone' is pron. indefinite and needs some clarification. That is, who can be this someone? And the answer is that he can be a scholar, a saint, an atheist, a pantheist, a fool, etc. The role of this 'someone' is seen in sub-str 1 (a) & (b) of str 2 in Part two, according to which he offers false claims, about 'wetness and vainness' of the experiences of life and even gives those claims a pattern. For instance, if one meets someone like St. Asharam, he will say that life can be meaningful (wet) only if one has 'guru' or else meaningless (vain). Then he will give examples of Rama, Mira, Vivekananda, etc., who had 'gurus.' Sub-str 1 of str two in part two is foregrounded as it doesn't have its parallel in part one. Anyway this part can be summed up thus : the poet has here tried to say that in the journey of life one may meet someone or may not meet anyone. It doesn't matter. The ultimate destiny of man remains the same, *i.e.*, 'vain.'

This ultimate destiny is further vividly projected through the parallelistic pattern that we see in sub-str 2 in part one and sub-str 2 of str two in part two, *viz.*, 'mouthful of breath on tomorrow's windowpane' and 'a maplike waterstain steaming upon a stone' respectively. Both the structures are foregrounded in their respective parts for their deviation from the earlier structures. Here we see the use of two images that realistically represent the ultimate truth of life. Let us examine both the images in some detail : Regarding the former, if one has mouthful of breath closing the lips tightly and then blows it on tomorrow's windowpane, it will make the glass wet and warm as well as opaque, and soon all this disappears. Here the poet has violated the selectional rule in 'tomorrow's windowpane.' It should have been something like 'tower's windowpane'. But then this way the poet has subtly juxtaposed the experiences of 'yesterday' and 'tomorrow.' That is, both are identical except that there is imaginative visualization of the things that have taken place in the case of the former, while that of the things that are yet to take place in the case of the latter. But the nature of the experiences in both the cases has been like 'a mouthful of breath on a windowpane', *i.e.*, initially warm, and meaningful but ultimately confused, cold and meaningless.

The latter image projects a flat stone with some water on its surface. Then this water slowly evaporates and leaves only a dry spot behind. That is, 'today' he met someone. Someone gave vainness of life experiences some shape and meaning. But then that too didn't make any difference. Now at the end of 'today' what he sees is the same *i.e.*, 'a dry spot of water on a stone', *i.e.*, the earlier warmth and meaningfulness is replaced by only memory spots. Thus, in both the images 'steam/vapour' is common which has two opposite qualities, *viz.*, wetness and warmth and opaqueness and transiency. And this is the truth of life. Man, while living his life through the wheel of yesterday-tomorrow-today, begins every experience in joy, warmth, meaningfulness, but then it starts getting clouded and finally ends in emptiness and nothingness. Ramanujan has thus told the ages old truth through fresh and fine images.

Parallelism can also be seen at the sound level which makes the whole poem compact, cohesive and memorable. Here we have instances of perfect rhymes like : met-wet, vain-pane-stain; imperfect rhymes like : met-it, mouth-breath; internal rhymes like : yesterday-today, no one-someone, etc., eye rhyme like : one-stone; alliterations like : was wet, was-vain, steaming upon a stone, today too, pretensions to a pattern; consonances like : but I met, steming upon a stone, it was wet; assonances like some one/s ^ m w ^ n/, wet n vein/ and so on.

The use of enjambment or the device of 'run on lines' has added one additional dimension to the poem. Let us have the poem with the use of enjambment :

Yesterday, I met ↵
no one :
it was wet ↵
and vain :
a mouth- ↵
ful of breath ↵
on tomorrow's windowpane.

And today too was vain.
But I met ↵
someone ↵
who gave it ↵
pretensions to a pattern :
a maplike waterstain ↵
steaming upon a stone.

Broadly enjambment has dual role to perform : one, it shows or rather gives the quality of motion to the poem, and two, it raises the reader's expectation which is either fulfilled or denied, and which in turn gives either shock, surprise, or further creates curiosity, and so on. A gliding glance at the use of enjambment above makes us see the thin stream like poem gliding onwards through short or full pauses and finally ends leaving an inexplicable satisfying silence behind. Every glide is faced with the element of shock or surprise. For instance, the opening line — 'yesterday, I met' has various possibilities for the next word, *e.g.*, a saint, a scholar, a friend, etc. But then one has the unexpected word 'no one'. In line No. 11 it is again 'But I met' and now the next word is 'someone'. Thus, the poem moves on from one shock or surprise to the next and ends at 'VT', *i.e.*, 'vainness' as terminus.

It is said that though Ramanujan wrote all his poetry while in America, India and Indian experiences remain the subject matter of his writing.[2] However, the present poem points to the fact that his subjects may appear to be Indian, but the spirit has been more in tune with the western philosophy of life. For instance, what the poet has talked of life goes closer to Shakespeare's vision, *viz.*, 'It (life) is a tale/Told by an idiot, full of sound and fury/signifying nothing.'[3] (*Macbeth*, V:5) On the other hand, the Indian view of life can be seen in our Upnishads. For instance, *Vruhadāranyaka Upnishad* reveals it through this small prayer :

asato mā sata gamaya
tamaso mā jyotirgamaya
mrityormā amrutama gamaya[4] (Vru-1 = 3 = 28)

Here the rishi has projected two aspects of life, *viz.*, 'asata' (transient, temporary) and 'sata' (changeless and permanent); 'tamas' (dark and ugly) and 'jyoti' (bright and beautiful); 'mrityu' (death and fearsome) and 'amrutam' (deathless, fearless, sweet). The western thinking is confined to only the former aspect, while the Indian philosophy looks upon life as a journey from the former to the latter. Ramanujan looks upon life as 'a mouthful of breath' blown 'on a windowpane' which highlights its ultimate reality as 'futility' and 'nothingness', while the prayer above points to life's ultimate reality as 'sata', 'jyoti' and 'amrutam.'

REFERENCES

1. *An Anthology of Indian English Poetry* : (ed.) by A Board of Editors (Calcutta : Longman, 1995), p. 44.
2. *Ibid.*, p. 76.
3. Shakespeare : *Macbeth* (ed.) J. Dover Wilson (Great Britain, UP, 1951), p. 79.
4. *Vruhadāranyak Upnishad* : (ed.) Pt. Shriram Sharma (Sanskriti Sansthan : Bareilly, 1991), p. 37.

5

Soul's Journey in Niranjan Mohanty's *Prayers to Lord Jagannatha*

—*D.C. Chambial*

The poet in the modern times, besides indulging in the process of creating something beautiful beyond what actually exists on this *terra-firma*, in the domain of his imaginative vision, keeps an eye on the society about himself, feels, enjoys and suffers like his fellow-beings. But, when such personal experiences are transfused with the imaginative sensibility of the poet, it is ennobled. Modern researches and inventions in physical and bio-sciences have shattered the orthodox religious dogmas and the man, now, has started questioning the existence and the omnipotence of God. With this shift in man's psyche, even the nature of prayers to the Lord Almighty has undergone a sea change-highly devotional attitude to highly sceptic attitude is manifested in Mohanty's *Prayer's to Lord Jagannatha.** This paper purposes to study soul's journey in these prayers.

The very first prayer begins with a request to the Lord of the universe to burn his breath before he could begin his prayers, and tear his tongue ere he could produce the unpleasant sound, so that the protagonist is made unable to voice his doubts about the Lord, who creates, protects, guides and destroys the universe. The very first stanza :

*The *Prayers to Lord Jagannatha* by Niranjan Mohanty, first published in Poetry, No. 11 (Jan. 1986) Aska, Orissa.

Oh Lord of the universe,
burn my breath before I pray,
tear out my tongue before I bray.[1]

suggests that he is not to praise and thank the Lord. Instead, he has certain doubts and grievances that question His omnipotence. The quite unusual words are bound to startle the reader. For, a staunch devotee never begins his prayers with or like the words used by Professor Mohanty, the poet of these prayers. The poet is apprehensive that he may be punished for his questioning His authority, using an abusive language and catechizing Him for His impuissance to protect the innocent from natural calamities and disasters and allowing moral debility in the society.

The protagonist takes the reader into confidence by telling him that he is never regular in his prayers. Occasional misfortune or illness in the family remind him of the Lord Jagannatha, and then, he prays either for the recovery of his family members from illness or to tide over the period of grief or misfortune. The words, "often when cornered by grief", tell very clearly about his remembering God. These words emphatically suggest his purpose of praying to Him. In his prayers, he is very simple and burns no "incense sweet/From chain-swung censor teeming."[2] He only burns incense-sticks and prays not in the morning but in the evening with eyes shut and body still, after the dull and drab toil of the day is over.

Thus, having enunciated the objective, mode and time of his prayers that serve like a background, the doubts begin to appear. The protagonist wonders who has made Him the Lord or "the mighty seer" (I, 8) of the universe and tells about his physical shape. Here, the protagonist seems the describe the shape of the statue of Lord Jagannatha, a cripple, without hands and feet.

The poet, through protagonist, takes the readers into the heart of ceremonies at the temple when crowd throng to offer their prayers amidst the priests' chanting of hymns. A noisy and boisterous world is created. The protagonist fails to know how the Lord can tolerate this noise that no human can tolerate.

He is either senseless or deaf, unable to hear the noise or a lot greater than the ordinary human beings to anull the effect of this noise that sets Him apart from the rest of humanity and makes Him Lord of the universe. But at the same time, the protagonist's imagination takes a swing and he begins to suspect His omnipotence :

> I don't exactly remember
> how many times you had been hidden
> and stolen and hidden, again and again? (II, 7-9)

These words are an eyeopener. The Lord, who is unable to defend Himself from thieves and plunderers, how can He defend, protect, cure and guide the mortal human beings. With this argument, the poet negates the supremacy and omnipotence attributed to the Lord by religious zealots. The protagonist has in mind the visible concrete shape of the statue of the Lord that is stolen and hidden for fear of being traced out. Here his mind is resonating between two worlds of faith and doubt. Should he express his faith in the Lord by completely resigning himself to the will of the Lord or not? When He Himself appears helpless before the thieves. It is not that the statue of the Lord had been hidden by thieves alone but also by His devotees/priests for fear of being attacked and taken as booty by plunderers. Thus, the protagonist calls Him a great coward and doubts why people worship so coward a deity. The impetus is heightened by designating Him "C' Lord" (II, 12) with a capital 'C' for cowardice.

Having expressed his suspicion, he apostrophises the Lord to press him with His third foot if his words delude and tease him :

> O Lord of the world
> press me down with your third foot,
> if I beguile you with lies or tease you. (II, 13-15)

The protagonist is quite convinced about the validity of his charges and propriety of his words.

In the third prayer, he becomes conscious of the atrocity of time symbolised by the ticking of the clock and calls it the invention only of a foolish head as this tick of the clock bores him greatly. The clock is described as the "cruel indicator of time." For being unable to keep pace with the time, the protagonist is admonished by his boss at office and his wife at home. His imagination is shuttling rapidly and the punctuality of time is yoked together with the correct pronunciation of words :

> My boss bangs me, if I'm late.
> My wife frowns at me, if I'm late.
> My daughter stares at me if I mispronounce a word.
> (III, 7-9)

The words 'bang' and 'frown', at once, concretize the angry outbursts of the boss and unwelcoming grimaces of the wife. He finds himself helpless at the hands of time and returns to Lord Jagannatha for some solace in his moments of utter confusion and helplessness. Now, he calls the Lord as the "Lord of suggestions" (III, 10). He seeks His suggestions to shun the fears that are continuously surging up in his mind — "the flourishing fears, day & night" (III, 12). His fears are nothing but that of being roughly treated by his boss at office and wife at home after the day's drudging work at his table. A feeling of disillusionment arise from wife's misunderstanding and boss's nonchalant attitude towards his helplessness. He becomes a cruel victim of time and misreckoning.

The Lord emerges as the Lord of suggestions by the poet's swinging back to the last stanza of the first prayer where the Lord withstands people abusing, grumbling, wheezing, weeping and praying around Himself, all at the same time. The protagonist seeks the same power that enables the Lord to withstand the terrible cruelty of time : "always ticking, ticking and ticking" (III, 6). The fear, whether he will be able to keep pace with it or lag behind, grips his mind. The time emerges as the barbarous thing which cares a fig for those who fail to keep pace with it.

In the fourth prayer the poet alludes to a myth from history — the king of Puri. The king and his brother, Balarama, ride horses to win the princess — "the quivering queen" (IV, 6), the daughter of a neighbouring king. The poet's imagination continues to move in a swing like motion, to and fro, but in resonance. Now, it swings back to massive car-dragging of the Lord Jagannath by one and all, irrespective of cast and creed. There is again an allusion to a lowborn devotee, Salbega, a Bauri, an untouchable, who was miles away praying to the Lord to enable him to take part in the car-dragging ceremony. His heart was pure like that of a child. The Lord hears his prayer and the car gets stuck in the sands. In spite of the optimum force exerted by the multitude to move it, it does not budge even an inch from its place until Salbega, whom the poet calls "half-Hindu half-Muslim" arrives there bare-footed and bleeding legs. He offers his coconut and joins hands with the multitude and the car moves.

The protagonist is abashed to see this multitude being drawn to the Lord's car. He thinks that the Lord must either be a great wizard who draws people to His car using some black magic or the people so drawn possess a heart "white like the morning's art." (V, 6) It is not the morning art by some other artist but morning is herself the artist. The image of serenity, quietude and sublimity of morning's art is imparted to the innocence, naiveté and eternal love of human heart. To people thus flooded into a homogeneous congregation, the poet asks the Lord if they who constitute this crowd are able to see "the fire burning with sacrosanct clarity/in the rotundity of your eyes" (V, 10-11) or are they all able to hear :

> the flute-songs, the conch-songs
> the echo of the horse feet
> in the prosiliency of your eyes? (V, 13-15)

The protagonist becomes sceptic of His dominant position. He is agonised to see the misery that scorches his heart's forest with "wild fire and fear of grief." (VI, 2) His this state of mental poise makes him lose propriety of words for a prayer and in hot temper he decides to abusive language for the Lord and tells Him not to take any action, for, that would redeem him and he doesn't long for redemption.... In fact, at the present moment, he doesn't seek any kindness from Him. He calls the Lord a 'murderer' (VI, 7), a 'thrawn thief' (VI, 10), and a 'precocious magician' (VI, 13). Here, there are direct references to the Lord Krishna who had murdered his uncle, Kamsa, to quench His heart's hibernating fervour. This is an act of Lord Krishna telling Arjuna the purpose of His taking birth in every age full of sins to redeem the pious, the indefatigable and the resolute in their duty — karma — and to destroy the sinners and the unrighteous. Lord Krishna says :

> Paritranaya sadhunam vinashaya cha dushkritam
> Dharmasamsthapanarthaya sambhavami yuge yuge.[3]

A "thrawn thief", because with the melodious tune of His flute He had stolen the hearts of the women of Gokula and Brindavana; a "precocious magician", when asked by His mother to open His mouth to see whether He had eaten soil : taking it to be the most appropriate time to reveal His true identity, He opened His mouth to leave His mother, Yashoda, dumb-founded to see the weird spectacle of the whole universe inside His mouth. He wanted to reveal His true identity to His mother and by performing this trick He fulfilled His objective and thus with this purposeful revelation He becomes the "precocious magician" in the ecstatic flux of poetic fancy.

The same figure of the Lord from the Hindu scriptures continues to haunt his imagination. In the seventh prayer the allusions are to saving Draupadi of her shame in the court of Duryodhana by Dushashana at the behest of his elder brother by unrobing her. Also, protecting an elephant from the jaws of a fatal crocodile. Besides these allusions to Lord Krishna, Lord Rama also appear momentarily in the relieving of Ahalya from the cursed stone shape and in the image "building bridges on the blue sea." (VII, 5) This allusion takes us back to the time when Lord Rama had built a bridge over the sea at Rameshvaram, bridging India and Srilanka during His march to invade Srilanka to emancipate His spouse, Sita, from Ravana's captivity. Before the spell of the prayer is over, the protagonist identifies himself with a flower in the Lord's garland or with His spouse, like the Sufis, and prays :

> Will you not make me a flower
> in the garland?
> Choose me to be your bride? (VII, 13-15)

He yearns to be in the Lord's eternal company in order to enjoy the bliss of His contact.

The eighth and ninth prayers exhibit poet's socio-consciousness in full measure. In the following lines :

> O, Lord
> Sitting still, unperturbed
> will you not grow fat? (VIII, 1-3)

Now, he has the Lord's statue before his mind's eye. The suggestion of God's action for the destruction of the evil and sin is also lurking simultaneously. How could a saviour of the universe sit still when "the children drown, loafers loot and lepers tremble." The images of black-lies, rats, bats and carrion-crows suggest the moral debility and social corruption. The ninth prayer is the heightened revelation of the poet's socio-consciousness about the present state of affairs. The poet's keen observation is microscopic in its nature and his pungent satire cuts with a scalpel precision through the hearts of the hypocrites. Let us read it for its complete impact :

> Pallid politicians pride over
> their past pastime.
> Ricksaw-pullers threaten strike.
>
> Teachers doze in the classrooms
> Professors choose angels
> to pluck their grey hair.
>
> Doctors demand bonus.
> Women denounce cooking.
> Engineers fancy on distant tours.
>
> Beggars refuse coins.
> Children refuse schooling.
> Lovers refuse dreaming.
>
> Prices rise. Potato out of stock.
> Salt, tagged as an export goods.
> The theatre-halls overflowing. (IX)

and prays Him to "cram us to your credence" (XI, 12) by "the dagger of your love" (XII, 3) to "denude us/when rains patter" (XII, 14). The poet's expectation to "Visit us/when the game is over" (XIII, 13-14) connotes on one hand Lord Krishna's revelation to Arjuna in the *Gita* the purpose of His taking birth at the ebb of dharma and at the tide of what is anti-ethical, antireligious, ignoble or in short adharma; on the other hand, the visit of Lord Vishnu to Vaivastava Manu, after the Great Flood, when everything else except he were destroyed. The purpose of the visit, shown in the very next line, is to "inject us with blood." That suggests that the generations of human qualities for the procreation of a healthy and sane race without any personal gall or prejudice, where the fountains of prosperity and peace sprinkle forth the elixir of a blissful life to transform the Earth into a Heaven.

In the penultimate prayer the atmosphere of resignation starts when the poet accentuates the intensity of seeking the Lord's blessing to enable him to see things in their absolute, the primordial virginal chastity, the original truth. The wish to become a cripple like the Lord Jagannatha's as revealed to us in the fourth stanza of the first prayer, the poet has begun to identify himself with the Lord's devotee, like Salbega, and prays to be one with Him. This identification is heightened in the similes of pollen and echo :

> Make me invisible like the pollen
> of a flower, make me humble
> like an echo. (XIV, 7-9)

The invisibility of the pollen and the humbleness of the echo both are suggestive of the godly stage to which the protagonist is striving. The image, "scatter me on your twenty-two steps," again implies the protagonist's humility to be one with Him like the dust beneath His feet. The fusion of the soul with God echoes the Vedic philosophy of *Atmaiva Pramatma*, the soul is the God.

In the last prayer the poet prays to the Lord to enclose humanity in the just, serene, soothing light of His eyes; begs of Him to instruct and guide at the time of difficulties like John

Henry Newman.[4] The politicians are mocked in the epithet 'half-monks' who deceive and 'mariners' who drown the people. The poet makes 'a jib at the politicians' lack of clear vision and policies to steer the nation on a limited perspective and the world at the larger one. He again and again prays to the Lord to raise him and the humanity from the present sad state to the state of eternal bliss : "Where the myth-makers open / the white pages of a bright almanac" (X. 14-15). The poet now reaches a stage when he prays to the Lord to bless the whole mankind with the eternal knowledge of "what was, what is and what will be" lying eternally in the "mytho-poeic corner of his eyes;" all should find poise and peace in chanting His name and identifying themselves with one another as the children of the same God. The poet is also conscious of his vocation as a poet and, therefore, prays to the Lord to inspire the whole mankind to learn the use of words and decipher the meaning of their oozing silence.

The first person pronoun 'I' undergoes metamorphosis as the poet reaches the tenth prayer into the first person plural 'us' that encompasses within its ambit the whole mankind fraught with eternal fear of moral perversion and atomic annihilation. For the catharsis of this fear he prays to the Lord to instil into the hearts of all men a fellow-feeling; a feeling to identify with the lowest of the low. This identification of one and all with the same gives birth to the spirit of '*Brahmoasmi*' and we are lead to the mythic belief of oneness. This 'us' grows in stature and significance in the prayers from ten to twelve. The poet also seeks the Lord's permission

> ...to pray
> beneath that lofty banyan tree
> where people tie wish-stones, year after year.
>
> (XIV, 13-15)

The banyan tree is considered religious and sanctimonious by the Hindus and the Buddhists. The poet, by praying under such a tree, yearns for the fulfilment of his own wishes — the eradication of all evils and poverty from the surface of this Earth.

The climax of the intensity of the prayers is reached in the fifteenth prayer in which the poet prays to the Lord to strengthen his

...bosom to bear the burden
the world shall plant; strengthen
my fingers to hold a pen.

Strengthen
me to crawl
out of the darkness. (XV, 1-6)

The pendulum like swinging movement of his thought is noteworthy. At first he wants to wear the burden of the world like a martyr but at the very next moment he becomes conscious of his vocation as a poet and prays to the Lord to strengthen his fingers to hold the pen to wage a war against the "half-monks", the "rats" and the "bats" to expose their hypocrisy. As an agent of the creative life-force, with the help of his pen, creates a world full fragrant and fair littered with the leaves of Lord's love. And then, in a concrete image prays to strengthen him to come out of the darkness of ignorance into the spiritual light. The process is not as easy as the flow of an arroyo. The word 'crawl' is symbolic enough to suggest the struggle of this transformation from spiritual darkness to spiritual light. He seeks the Lord's blessing so that...in the winter of my moving years/I will net warmth from your eyes (XV, 11-12).

The journey of soul, in the prayers, starts with a modern man's tendency of being awfully busy and always falling behind time and a sense of protest at the inability of the Lord to protect the righteous, honest, innocent, and even His own statue. His atheistic frenzy is short-lived and soon he prays Lord to punish him for casting aspersions on His existence and omnipotence. Finally, he yearns to be one with the Lord. This sea-saw movement of the poet's doubt and faith in the Lord continues prayer after prayer. He comes to believe that He is the puppet-player and human beings are mere puppets dancing at His behest, He does not like the religious poets of the past, renounce everything to sing His glory, but, is very much conscious of his society, its evil and hypocrisy of man. All these doubts and fears give way to hope and he finds the real solution and blissful solace in the Lord. His faith undergoes transformation and swings more and more towards the Lord Jagannatha to such an extent that he becomes a true devotee, a recluse for whom the Lord is the only saviour and source. Despair and pessimism give way to hope. Without Him everything is dark and dismal and with the Lord it is lively, bright and cheerful.

The poet has, in these prayers, tried to reveal the reality "which is hidden below the surface and not yet been discovered and not only fixed and established connections but also the way the world moves and develops."[5] The poet concludes that to "this strange disease of modern life / with its sick hurry and divided aims"[6] the true solution lies only in resigning completely to the will of the Lord by establishing a rapport with Him. The poet, in the course of these prayers, emerges as a socio-conscious, religious and realist with whom we, the readers, experience, suffer and turn towards the Lord for the solution of all the ills of this world.

NOTES AND REFERENCES

1. Niranjan Mohanty, *Prayers to Lord Jagannatha*, 1, 1-3. All subsequent references to the prayers have been incorporated in the text itself. The Roman numerals refer to prayer number and Arabic numerals refer to lines.
2. *Ode to Psyche*, John Keats, 32-33.
3. *The Gita*, IV, 8.
4. The poem under reference is *Lead, Kindly Light* wherein he prays :

   Lead, kindly Light, amid the encirching gloom,
   Lead Thou me on;
   The night is dark, and I am far from home;
   Lead Thou me on.

5. M. Khrapchencko, *The Writers Creative Individuality and Development of Literature* (Progress Publishers : Moscow, 1977), p. 20.
6. Matthew Arnold, "The Scholar Gypsy", II. 203-4.

6

Sailendra Narayan Tripathy's Poetry and his Post-modernist Leanings

—*D. Gnanasekaran*

Classicism is orderly and one-sided truth. Classicism in art seeks to invest the universal with beauty. Classicism is objective, and not subjective, in the sense that the conceptions are derived from the world of impressions. "This objectivity gives the classical art and literature an element of aloofness from the jarring and conflicting elements of life" (George 1971 : 136). Classicism, therefore, is beautiful but incomplete. Modernism is nothing but the crystallization of classicism. It is post-modernism that attempts to explode the well-guarded tradition and to explore the possibilities of bringing back the marginalised into the ambience of human perception and analysis. It reveals the other side of truth. Of course through the ages, the status-quo-ists have mostly controlled the State and marginalised the wisdom of those who broke away from the existing contemporary spirit and refused to compromise their path-finding democratic sensibility. Such innovative-spirited men were cast aside as tearaways by their majority fellowmen. But sooner or later, the marginalised wisdom has found acceptance within the mainstream, and unleashed a long process of change. Sailendra Narayan Tripathy was inescapably caught in this process of changing perceptions in the domain of creative writing.

The marginalised is often condemned as "ugly" but it is, no doubt, an integral part of beauty. Both the centralised and the erstwhile marginalised keep company now and the reader is able to see the entire gamut of mundane action with all its permutations and combinations. The suppressed, rather willingly hidden surfaces now in the poetry of an Indian English poet, S.N. Tripathy who is a post-modernist in his outlook. A host of writers, poets in particular, try to suppress the so-called "ugly" though it is bursting to the seams emotionally and bleeding surrealistically. But here is an honest soul that strives to see life in its totality with all its deficiencies and limitations. To many who go through Tripathy's poems collected under the title *I am Phallic God and Other Poems*, he may appear odd and sometimes even repulsive. As a characteristic post-modernist, he is quite outspoken and bold in depicting matters relating to man-woman relationship.

Sex is not an anathema in life. The Indian ethos of life is broadly based on the conceptions, the *purushaarthas* and *the ashramas*, which lie at the root of the Indian way of life. *Purushaarthas* mean the objectives of life. The *purushaarthas* to be lived are *Dharma, Artha*, and *Kama* with a view to obtaining *Moksha*, the ultimate objective. *Dharma* clearly is not religion here, but the way of life preserved in the *dharma sastras*. It covers not only ethics but also morality as understood in society. *Artha* means material welfare, *not* accumulation of wealth, but *soubhagya*, material happiness and general prosperity. The third *purushaartha*, *Kama* or the life of the sense was equally an essential part of Indian culture. Though *Kama* literally means desire, love, etc., in the context of *Dharma*, *Artha* and *Kama*, it signifies physical and artistic enjoyment, the life of the senses in its widest aspect. The man-woman relationship is symbolic of the relationship of *purusha* and *prakriti* from which creation itself issued forth. It is therefore something of the nature of a sacrament. The normal satisfaction of the senses, *kama*, was therefore considered a *purushaartha* on the same footing as *dharma* and *artha*. It was a balance between the three that the Indian culture aimed at.

So sex is not something that one should abhor or shrink from discussing it with others. Tripathy's exaggeration of sensuality is nothing but the excision of the septic part of a lacerated soul before the remedial treatment begins. Tripathy's soul is lacerated and it bleeds and the smell of fresh blood emanates from his poetry. He says in his Foreword : "My poetry is the poetry of the loins. They have directly flowed from the loins without grammar, without inhibition. Therefore my poetry is dark, primitive, passionate, a little diabolical." He proclaims himself to be "truthful, honest and candid." He does not believe in "circumlocution, shibboleth or shenanigan." In his poetry the marginalised stages a comeback. To the classical, slavish mind, his poems are really as diabolical as the poet claims them to be. If one asks "Hey! What are they?", the poet would answer with the borrowed words, "Nay, these are but the wounds of love." So the wounds are there as they are and as they ought to be. One may twist one's nose, raise one's eyes, bite one's lip, push down a lump of saliva at the sight of the fresh bleeding wound, but a wound is a wound. You close your eyes in sheer disgust and hold your tongue in shock. All your hypocritical actions cannot keep you off the wound and the truth can never be concealed forever. The poet tries to unfold the mystery and in the process he is edgy, erotic, mystical and death-obsessed.

Apples, blossoms, flowers, petals, loins, groins, windows, bones, lips, day, night, flesh, blood, life, death, thighs, birds, rainbow and so on — all these images crisscross his agony of life which manifests in the warp and the woof of his poetry. The poet is haunted by one 'S' inconsolably and he feels like the child "wriggling in the darkness of her womb" while

Dews were falling everywhere
On the breasts of the night.

(*Farewelling A Lady With Dews in September*)

Of all her attractions that lure him and every other man, the blackmole on her right cheek is a bait

To hook handsome young poets
And hack them to death.

(*Hamlet Was No Fool*)

Again, her blackmole looks like a dream island
Where i try to catch God's rainbow.

(*Two Faces By Dimlit Candle*)

Unrequited love leads to disenchantment. The suppressed desires transform into hungry wolves and consume the very sap of his being of a lover in him :

You're a river when I drop a stone
There is no ripple on the water
You're a night dark as blood
I search for the moon
Until I'm eaten by the wolves of desire.
(*To A Strange Lady*)

Such passions of the poet "bark like dogs of the night" (*There In The Park*) and drive the poet mad to redefine the concept of woman parodying Shakespeare, "Cruelty thy name is woman." The poet loved the girl with a vengeance but his love was not reciprocated. The love failure escalated into an emotional outburst and an experience beyond the parameters of human comprehension. The cry of his agonizing soul is epitomized and has thus manifested in these lines :

He loved life
Life never loved him. (*When I Lie Gently Dead*)

Being another "La Belle Dame Sans Merci", his 'S' doesn't

...hesitate to drink
From the bloodless poet
Who had blood for ink. (*A Letter to Fanny Brawne*)

The "Butcher Honey" representing 'S' can rather eat his soul and drink his poetry to highlight her highhanded profile. The poet likens man's endeavour of fathoming the woman's heart to a life-long exploration and if he succeeds in it, it is his lifetime achievement. But often the exploration bears no fruit since a lifetime is not enough to reach the inscrutable bottom of the woman's heart :

Women are often lonely, lost islands in the sea
Men are explorers
Exploring is often life-long. (*Men*)

Tripathy takes upon himself the task of a social critic and his critical cannons are launched at bastards breeding "young bastards." Bastard children are as legitimate as "pure products" and the purity of one's birth is a matter of faith and acceptance. How shamelessly proud we are in classifying the products of physical communion without knowing where exactly we belong.

The poem *Give My Regards to Dad* dramatizes the situation where the so-called "illegitimate child" has every right to call his dad a bastard.

Tripathy at times goes poetically 'mad' and his imagination runs riot. Colours of rainbow are splashed but all colours of the physical manifestations realized in his poetry inevitably refract from the medium of his wounded soul. There is a purpose in his madness and there is a lesson in his diabolical exposition, characterized by abundant frankness, but not to kindle our baser instincts. His horrid expositions are a pointer to the degrading society wrapped up in materialism and the increasingly disintegrating moral system. Man, with his sixth sense, is able to X-ray a woman through just his naked eyes and he is also able to wax eloquent of feminine virtues. Tripathy's poetry is a sort of poetic version of the Freudian/Jungian perception that scans the turbulent soul of cunning men and fallen women. Basically a man or woman is a bundle of emotions governed by sexual instincts. But sexual instincts themselves in turn must be conditioned by the basic ethics of life. His poems seem to be a kind of life-conditioner paving the way for a healthy co-existence of the sensual and the spiritual.

Besides the one-sided, soul-eating love, death is another recurring theme in Tripathy's poems. Gloom persists and the shadow of death looms large in his poetic jottings about the ever-eluding puzzle of life. Two things fill the poet's mind with ever new and increasing admiration and awe — the woman's heart and the meaning of life which is decisively circumscribed by death. The philosophy of life, to the poet, is also an irony of life :

God is the loneliest animal
Therefore has created the world
And more lonely now. (*Loneliness*)

We are puzzled whether God has alienated Man or Man has distanced himself from God for the latter's indifference to the human sufferings. When his grandfather coughed blood, the poet put cotton in his ear and offered prayers to God for his speedy death (*You, Grandfather*). In a way, death is a most welcome guest to end our sufferings, especially those of terminal patients. The poet indicts himself for being callous and admits his being a victim of modern life devoid of humanism and aim. Each of Tripathy's poems is not a rosy picture of life but a grim picture in words of harsh reality. Reality cannot be dismissed but is often disguised. Tripathy tears up the disguise to shreds vehemently, turns the inside out and bares the human diabolical psychological matrix. Man is a Phallic God and is unavoidably caught in the vicious web of sex. He feels that Man and Woman together lost Eden and "came down to spoil to whatever was in this heaven" (*Men*).

The question 'What's agony?' which is also the title of a poem evades all our attempts to define "agony" and the meaning is not reached all too soon. The poet brings before our eyes a collage of both the realistic and the imaginative to illustrate *agony* through a word picture :

> When a dead man was carried in a procession
> His wife semi-naked howling like jackal in my village
> Her innocent breasts looking like babies crying for milk.

The heart-rending scene cannot better be depicted in the Indian context than the poet does here. His poetic images are both highly suggestive and woefully poignant. His imagery is at its best in the following lines from the poem '*Can't Stop Loving You*' :

> Each time I saw sunshine straight in your eye
> Like an insect I wanted to hold the naked flame in
> my hands and die.

Widowhood in India is clothed in white symbolizing purity and accorded social sanctity. But a widow's green memories and greener feelings torment her entire being. Here is a widow's prayer :

> You took my youth
> all my fire
> now take me Lord
> under your care. (*A Prayer*)

A mother lost her child and her cry in the night creeps into, and chills, our blood and we feel worms zigzag their way into our heart. Her soul bleeds :

> My child
> Can't you feel in the tomb
> Pains of my empty womb,
> The pains of a failed feminity. (*A Cry In The Night*)

The mother watered her child Bablu for ten months. She bore the child as her flower on her boughs and as the fruit of her loins. So naturally she can't but cry piercing the stillness of the night over the unexpected and untimely loss.

Every action is predetermined and so God must be a sadist who prescribes everything for everyone. This theory of predeterminism and destiny is our last cry in despair. Man is subdued and forced to swallow his defeat philosophically when he seems to have been hopelessly seized of the problem of getting out of a certain predicament :

> Life is a movie
> You can't know
> The goodie from the baddie. (*Baby*)

The poem *Welcoming New Year* is a faithful document of our shameless sophisticated "adjustments" with which we make our way out of our "burnt soul and burnt dreams" to seek a way to thrive at any cost.

Life can never be without the nuances of differences, the marginalised peripheries or the ambiguous gray areas. To have everything that is black and white would eliminate the region of the unknown, the chanced upon. All boundaries have to be tested and parameters pushed. Symbolism is a technique used to have a penetrating vision into the unknown beyond the apparently existing horizons for further clarification and newer aesthetic exploration. Tripathy's poetry is largely wrought with a diabolical symbolism, an offshoot of post-modernism. Such symbolism shocks our poetic sensibility and strikes the nail of stark reality on the head by an alarming suggestiveness. To him, poetry

> Music — it was
> Lilting from the loins...

It was flowing everywhere
As if I was menstruating. (*Poetry*)

But symbolism here is deliberately twisted and the twist deconstructs our psychological make-up seething beneath the facade of hypocrisy. The poem '*The Cow and I*' demolishes the thin, already dilapidated barrier between humans and animals in the context of cross-cultural moorings. The poet succeeds in depicting that life is a continuous adjustment of internal relations to external affairs. Tripathy confesses that he is the Phallic God and he has the guts to admit it through a post-modernist diagnosis of life now. He ultimately leads one to a point of self-introspection and soul-rejuvenation and seems to convince us that man, even in the face of odds, with a resilience steeled by his determination to turn misfortune into salvation for himself and similarly affected people can never be defeated but destroyed.

REFERENCES

1. Tripathy, S.N. 1989. *I Am Phallic God and Other Poems*. Berhampur. Poesie Publications. (All the poetic lines quoted in the paper are from this edition).
2. George, A.G. 1991. *Studies in Poetry*. New Delhi : Heinemann.
3. Gnanasekaran, D. 1992. "The diabolical poetry of S.N. Tripathy." *Poetcrit* (Jan. 1992, 1) Maranda.
4. Pandit, M.P. 1989. *The Indian Spirit*. Pondicherry : Dipti Publications.

7

Humour and Irony : A Study of Dr. P. Raja's Poetry

—*K.V. Raghupathi*

Indian poetry in English is hundred and fifty years old. During this long period it has passed through many difficult phases to gain due recognition in the world. It has encountered many rough weathers before it has come to say. It has now entered into a world of new experiments, new insights, mores and techniques. Today, it has a new identity and distinct voice.

The sixties of the twentieth century saw the emergence of "New poets." They include Ezekiel, Jussawalla, Das, Mehrotra, Ramanujan, Patel, Nandy and so on, who have been duly recognised and acknowledged of their contributions. Today, across the sub-continent many poets are practising this art and every major and medium city and town can boast itself of having poets writing in English or bilingual poets. To this extent poets in English in India are largely urbanised. They may be called as "city poets." Dr. P. Raja is no exception to them. He lives in Pondicherry. He is a well-known Indian poet in English. Born in 1952, he has been writing over a period of eighteen years. A prolific writer, his poems, articles, short stories, one act plays, book reviews and features have appeared in a large number of periodicals in India and abroad. He is a recipient of Literary Award from Pondicherry University, International Eminent Poet Award from Chennai and Michael Madhusudan Academy Award from Kolkata. Dr. Raja has so far published a little more than three hundred poems in journals both in India and abroad. His first volume of poems, *From Zero To Infinity* containing fifty-two poems was published in 1987. His second volume *To The Lonely Grey Hair* comprising another fifty-two poems was brought out by him recently in September, 1997 after a gap of ten years.

Raja's poetry is primarily a poetry of humour mixed with irony, of humour expressed with ease and felicity, of feelings expressed concretely and clearly and not laconically and abstractly. There is no inhibited quality about his poetry. He just lets himself go in his poems. His is a free style; and he has not formulated any theory of his own. Yet, he has his own views and perceptions on what constitutes a poem. He poses this question : "What is a poem after all?" He answers : "The more we think about it, the less we know." In spite of it, in a characteristic way, he gives his own definition of what a poem is in one of his essays, "My Poems and I." He says : "Any piece of work in a definite form that gives cerebral pleasure is a good poem. It need not follow any of man-made rules. Like wind, a good poem breaks all barriers.... Hence my formula for a good poem is : A fertile poet + A fallow idea = a good poem." One may agree or disagree with his formula, but one has to agree with him when he says : Nobody's word is final. No one's uttering is law, when it comes to literature, the world of lovable lies." And he asserts with conviction : "No poet has written 100% good poems. No poetaster has written 100% bad poems."

The birth of a poem, according to Raja, involves a painful process which every poet undergoes. He presents this process in his poem, "Birth of a Poem" in which he compares the pain involved in it with that of the pain experienced by a pregnant woman from the stage of conception to the moment of delivery.

The poet writes :

> Labour pain in the cerebrum.
> Slight literary bleeding.
> Ah! Indescribable horror.
> Slowly, fairly and sprightly
> peeps the child of the brain.
> Crying and pushing it makes its way.

A careful medicated wash
and it glistens. (*From Zero to Infinity*, p. 14)

As the poem is created, Raja says, it provides immense relief and joy to the poet.

Lo! Unaccountable bliss
the mother enjoys
to see the poem trotting the globe
with the umbilical cord uncut forever.
(*From Zero to Infinity*, p. 14)

His poems deal with a variety of subjects. They present a spectrum of life, from birth to death. His poetry is distinctly marked by humour, irony and satire. He is at his best in entertaining the readers. At the same time his sense of humour is tinged with an acute sense of meaning which generally a casual reader misses and a serious reader captures with a sense of imagination and understanding. Modestly, he calls himself an entertainer. He writes : "Primarily I am an entertainer. The eighteen years of experience I have on my back as a language teacher has taught me the art of entertaining others. My secondary purpose is to show you the world through my eyes, perhaps with a tinge of imagination. I want to show you something that you nod your head with a smile or grit your teeth in contempt. Either way I have succeeded in evoking a response from you." (*For Your Ears Only*, p. 102)

"To The Lonely Grey Hair" is an ode full of humour and irony. Holding it between his forefinger and thumb, he addresses

I oiled you.
Now and then
shampooed you
and kept you always trim.
(*From Zero to Infinity*, p. 42)

But the hair has turned "unfaithful" to him. He questions : "Who bribed you, O hair!/to change your colour?" The lonely grey hair is now unwanted for the poet. So also, ironically, the poet says that the dishonest and the unfaithful have no place in his life.

The dishonest and the unfaithful
deserve no place in my realm.
Out you go
O, my one-time friend and now my foe.

(*From Zero to Infinity*, p. 43)

But years later the poet was again disturbed by many grey hair. They all seemed to ask him with a vengeance : "Hei you! Puller of the lonely grey hair! What can you do now?" He was sure he would turn bald if he ventured to pull all of them out. This disturbance forced him to write a poem, "To The Poet From his Hair." The hair complain to the poet that they are not his slaves to dance to his comb.

To change colours
is our birthright.
And you can't stop us
from bidding adieu to you
when we feel like doing so.

You have no right to call us
'dishonest', 'unfaithful' and
above all 'bribed.'

Apologise and behave yourself,
lest we should desert you
with our kith and kin
and give pension to your comb.

(*To the Lonely Grey Hair*, p. 11)

By writing this poem the poet made fun of himself. He loved humour and he wanted to share it with others. He writes : "Having learnt to laugh at myself, how can I let others off scot-free? Humour is the salt of existence. And what is satire without humour?"

"A Doubt Cleared" is yet another piece of humour tinted with satire on his guru, Professor N. Santhalingam, the man who initiated the poet into the art of writing. The Professor is a profound possessor of a well-equipped library, a genius, well learned in the literatures of the world, his knowledge is partly accessible to his students and mostly inaccessible to his colleagues. The poet was once his student. Had the poet not become his colleague, he would still continue to enjoy the privilege of learning a lot from him. But alas! he wrote this poem :

What are pillow-like dictionaries
and rows of voluminous encyclopaedias for?
Refer to them and clarify your doubt.

It's not that I do not know.
But why do you want me to do it for you?
Every fruit the fruit of hard labour.

Knowledge is not cheap as you think.
Certainly not as cheap as tap-water.
It's well-water in mid-summer.

I can only tell you where the well is.
Don't expect me to bale out Water for you.
Even if I do, will it ever be your own?

(*To The Lonely Grey Hair*, p. 37)

Raja has written two excellent poems on academic seminars and discussions. "Seminar" is an excellent satirical poem. In it the poet ridicules the usual sapless academic seminars in universities. Indeed, this poem created ill-will and enmity among some academicians. The poet confesses that two journals ran by two different universities rejected the poem, but an international monthly published it very prominently in one of its special issues. The poem contains the following lines :

Cups and saucers
vie with each other
to kiss the lips of participants.

Shawls and garlands,
Clicking cameras and
blinding flash-lights
stir up their pride.

Encomiums — a mutual affair —
drench them to the bones.
Every fellow is a lord on the dais.

Listen to my trumpet.
Too....toot.....toot.

Trees have roots.
Crows have wings.
2+2 make four.

Listen to my big drum.
Bang....bang....bang.

Hands clap....hands shake hands.
Hands pat shoulders. Lips praise.
Hearts fume. Teeth grit.

Ba.....ba......Black sheep!
Have you any wool?
No Sir, No Sir!
No bag is full. (*To The Lonely Grey Hair*, p. 58)

The satire finds further expression in another poem "Refresher Course." His humour is clear, more explicit, penetrating and biting. This is comparatively a long poem.

Silence.
The Resource Person has arrived
to talk to you of
Derida, Foucault and Said.

Silence.
Did you get your folder,
a sheaf of papers and a ball pen?
Don't fail to get your name registered
at the office of the Director.
That assures you of your D.A. and T.A.

Silence.
The R.P. is a genius, an authority
on Modern criticism.
Widely travelled, well-read
he can deliver his lectures
keeping no notes in hand.
Please listen.

"At what time do we break for tea?
Remind me when it is time. I'll stop.
I am accustomed to non-stop lectures.
Now to Derrida, Foucault and Said.
I was with them in their homes.

Thanks to U.G.C.
Derrida's daughter is good-looking.
Foucault's mother is homely.

Said's wife is a fine host.
In fact they plan a trip to my home.
I think it is time to break for lunch.
Perhaps we can meet after
a couple of hours to discuss
Deconstruction."

"Hei, you there! Get me
a glass of hot water.
I am damn scared of cholera."

"Why the hell is there no salt
in the curd? Get me a spoonful.
Damn with the cook."

"Too many stones in
every mouthful of rice. Scoundrels!
Should they feed us like beggars?"

Silence please.
Please listen.

"What shall we" do now?
Afternoons are sleepy.
Oh! we have to do deconstruction.
Deconstruction is not construction.
Construction is not deconstruction.
Do you catch my point?
Am I making myself clear to you?
Deconstruction is...
Is there a tea-break in the afternoon?

By the bye please check up
if my payment is ready.
I've reserved a seat in the 5 o'clock bus.
Tomorrow I must go to the State University
to lecture on the Feminist Movement.

How many here support the movement?

Thank you. Please feel free
to write me if you have doubts
in Derrida, Foucault and Said.
Let their tribe increase.
We will grow rich.
Thanks to U.G.C.
Be inspired by the lectures
I've delivered.
Teach your students well.
Ours is the noblest of professions.
Will some one drop me at the bus stop?
I must catch the 5 o'clock bus.
Good by.... The world is round.
See you again somewhere.

(*To The Lonely Grey Hair*, pp. 30-2)

Dr. Raja is an unromantic poet. His satire is incisive, but quite harmless if it is taken in the right spirit. It fits every man. "Whomsoever the cap fits, let them wear it," he says. "We Indians" is a poem both satirical and ironical in tone. In it the poet laughs at those "weeping philosophers" who are eternally preoccupied with life before birth and life after death and not about life here on the earth. The last stanza is full of irony, penetrative and thought-provoking.

Do not ask us what about
life between birth and death.
We have no time for all that.

And you don't need an Indian
to answer such a simple question.

(*From Zero to Infinity*, p. 61)

Like other modern Indian English poets Raja wrote poetry with irony. But his irony is not saturated, as though a supreme poetic path for him. His irony goes with humour. They are inseparable in Raja's poetry. Limerick is a type of humorous poem with five lines, the first two rhyming with the last. Raja has written one such "Limerick" which is full of laughter.

There was a young man of Pondicherry
Who never went to bed without a cherie.
When he was asked why
He felt very shy.
And one day he was found in a dispensary.

The three daughters of a grand old man
Treated their father as an unwanted man.
But when he died
All of them cried
To save themselves from the ghost of the man.

A short sighted soldier with a bottle of gin
Went to the war-front in order to win.
Finding no soldier to fight
He started flying his kite.
And gave his foes a chance to sin.

A fat Indian old lady
Drank mugs and mugs of toddy.
One-two-three-four.

She gulped-she swore.
And lashed everyone with language bawdy.

There once was a man named Old John, the Bold,
Who kicked all those who said he was old.
When his wife dragged him
Just to kiss him
He cried he was very old.

(*From Zero to Infinity*, pp. 33-4)

"To a Mosquitoe" is not only satirical but metaphorical in its significance. In it the poet used mosquitoe as a metaphor for the exploiter who swindles and swells at the expense of the weak.

How well with your charming song
you mesmerize mankind!
Oh! Scrounger of man's fuel.

We toil and sweat.
We pay and eat.
Yet our bread is not a full loaf.

You stray and sing.
You swindle and swill.
And you swell well.

(*From Zero to Infinity*, p. 48)

"My Wife is a Scientist" is yet another example for his humour. He calls his wife "a Scientist" and "The kitchen is her laboratory." She minces; she chops;/she bakes; she broils;/ she serves; O, she serves!" The poem ends with the poet calling himself "her guinea pig." (*To The Lonely Grey Hair*, p. 41)

Raja's humour transcends all limitations. There is no mystery in it. Neither is it bloated with too much imagery. It is simple to the core. There is nothing obscurity that needs hard deciphering. His humour is devoid of all ornamentation; it is pure; one can easily understand as it tickles senses to laughter. In the poem, "She is Gone" the poet expresses his uneasyness and restlessness when he is left alone without his wife. The restlessness and boredom experienced by a husband during the absence of his wife is quite vexous and common. The poet expresses it most beautifully with a salt of laughter.

> I know
> I'll be alone.
> When she is gone.
>
> I'll have to cook my food
> and scratch my back.
> I'll have to wriggle in bed
> craving for the warmth
> she gave me all these years.
>
> I know
> I'll miss
> her charming, shining face
> pressing against the windowpane
> awaiting my return home.
>
> I know
> I'll miss
> the evening snacks and hot tea
> sprinkled with a solacing smile.
>
> I know
> my parched lips will crack
> in the absence of
> her cool affectionate kiss.
>
> I know
> I'll be alone
> digging my memories and
> smiling at them all the time
> awaiting her message and her call.

(*To The Lonely Grey Hair*, p. 29)

In a beautiful poem, "Yama, Lord of Death" the poet says that no body can escape from "Him." "His decision is final/ His buffalo is no blind animal./His noose knows its way." "Your fat savings in Swiss Banks,/your gold and diamonds in Lockers/ can't bribe Him to shut His eyes." "Your prayers and prostrations,/your sweet-smelling flowers and joss sticks/can't tempt Him to grant you a reprieve./No, not even a panegyric in pleasing verse." "The gruesome barrels of AK-56s/can't snap His all-powerful noose./No, not even your acid bomb-shells." Then, what shall one do? The poet says humorously : "Surrender them, with a smile/writ large on your face./Have no fear, no, not in the least,/for Yama is another Brahma."

"In Fools and God" the poet presents his encounters with his wife and father, how each calls him 'fool' and 'God' interchangeably for what he does. He writes "Fools and God,/ I think,/can interchange/in this riddle of a manifold world." The poem "Love" castigates vulgarity and bawdiness. It symbolises the false love. It shows how modern man has lost its true sense in his sheer pursuit of pleasures from the flesh.

> What do they do there,
> making a gentle music
> — falling and rising?
>
> Oh! They are poets
> making a poem
> — a festival in the flesh.
>
> Oh! They are musicians
> composing a lullaby
> — a refrain in the miracle play.
>
> Oh! They are butchers
> interested in the meat.
> They feel each other's weight.
>
> Ah! Do they call it love?
> Lewd Tom! Bawdy Tabby!
> 'Love' is a four-letter word.

(*To The Lonely Grey Hair*, p. 42)

In another poem "In Indian Streets", the poet is moved by the picture of ordinary but enduring life experienced by "naked urchins/clamouring for sundal given at the temple/by sinners seeking redemption;" "thirsty women/quarrelling over their seniority/ in the que at the street tap"; "the angry old men/shouting at the ration-shop dealer/for displaying empty palm-oil cans"; "the disappointed young men/raising slogans against the government/ for not activating the Employment Exchange Office;" "the wee ones with empty stomachs/crying for a cup of milk, when cauldrons of it/wash the dirt off the sacred stones." At the end, the poem becomes ironical in tone and the poet is so disgusted that he expresses in revulsion that the crying in the streets must be the gods themselves/screaming for their safety/from bullet-battered temples." The recollection is picturesque and vivid. (*To The Lonely Grey Hair*, p. 44)

"Oh, These Ideas" is a poem in two stanzas. There are both wanted and unwanted ideas jostling and cramming together in the poet's mind. In the first stanza the poet is restless with the constantly troubling ideas.

> Where do these ideas come from?
> Why do they get crammed in my skull
> and ram it for an outlet?
> Can't they have patience
> and warm their way through?
> What a riot is going on in there!
> Should I run mad or blow my brains out?
>
> (*To The Lonely Grey Hair*, p. 50)

In the second stanza the poet feels the emptyness of mind. He longs for new ideas which have become quite elusive.

> Where did these ideas go?
> What must I do to get them?
> My skull seems to be empty.
> It's a beggar's bowl now.
> Can't they take pity on me?
> I long for a shower. My roots are dry.
> Should I have cups or lips or books?
>
> (*To The Lonely Grey Hair*, p. 50)

In "Quiz Master", the poet tells us that "The Quiz master/ is no genius/with extraordinary talents/to be wondered at." "Allow him no credit at all./Find for yourself how he fumbles without those blessed sheets." At the end, the poet says, "Quiz is a mere game of cards/where chance plays a major role/while talent only a minor one./The master is no Ace but only a joker." (*To The Lonely Grey Hair*, p. 52)

Raja's humour is not dry and sapless. It is full of life and vivacious. He has not written poems on abstruse and mystifying things. On the contrary, his poems are concrete representations of his own experiences in his day-to-day life. His experiences are quite mundane, very much earthly and human. "The Child" brings out the immediate and the present and not the remote, obscure and incomprehensible. The little boy is eager to know who god is but lands himself in the kitchen smacking his lips and sees god in his mother who offers him "fillets of fried fish peppered with grace and love." (*To The Lonely Grey Hair*, p. 57)

"Who is God?"
asked the child,
"about whom everyone speaks
but no one knows."

"He is the one who
created fish in the sea
and in the river,"
replied the Theist.

"No," retorted the Atheist
"He is the one who
invented net and
fishing rod."

Baffled stood the child.

"Come on, you child,"
called the mother from the kitchen.
"What have you to do
with those idlers? Come on."

The child rushed to her and
from her kind hands took
fillets of fried fish
peppered with grace and love.

The child smacked his lips and
saw God in his mother.
(*To The Lonely Grey Hair*, p. 57)

"The Bald" is ludicrous and amusing. In it he writes :

Who has unmaned the lion?
What ill wind blew
uprooting the crown of crops,
leaving no trace?
What curse has come
and passed
leaving the cock uncombed?
What plague is this?
A whole forest
is notoriously laid waste,
All is quiet. All is still.
There is silence from nape to brow.
(*To The Lonely Grey Hair*, p. 61)

In "Get Lost, You Cynic" the poet lambasts the cynic who questions him about his popularity of his writings. It is true, the poet admits unashamedly that he cannot write like Kafka or Camus. By saying this, Raja declares openly and plainly that he is not a serious writer, in the sense that his poetry does not include the most serious and complex things of human life. His is simple, ordinary and common. He honestly justifies the reason of his zeal in writing poetry. He writes because, "I have a fire in me/that keeps on pushing my pen." The poet further gives a fitting reply to such cynics who question his authenticity and simplicity. He writes :

All may not produce a Mona Lisa Gioconda.
But there are painters around.
All may not produce a Venus de Milo.
But there are sculptors around.

All may not produce an Effel Tower.
But there are engineers around.
All may not produce a Cleopatra.
But there are fathers around.
Aren't you a father, Sir?
Or are your daughters as ugly as you are?

(*To The Lonely Grey Hair*, p. 60)

Dr. Raja is not a confessional poet like Kamala Das, nor a poet of pure intellectualism like Shiv K. Kumar. He is a poet of communication like Ezekiel, more essentially a poet of humour. Humour is the staple diet of his poetry. His humour is not directed against any individual. He has always aimed at the common, or sometimes unusual, odd and exotic. His sense of humour is untarnished by the excess of images and metaphors. His humour is plain, simple and unostentatious. Though Raja carries a sense of humour in all his poetry, it is never bereft of meaning. Each poem ends with a note of irony. The meaning is concealed, and it is sharp and acute.

It is notable that Raja has presented the humour objectively and crisply. It is most appealing because of the implied empathy and pathos. He is at his best in provoking a sense of laughter. The poems in *From Zero to Infinity* and *To The Lonely Grey Hair* present an integrated experiences of his life in the mundane world with felicity and ease. The poems amply testify his quality of fancy, imagination and reflection. He wrote in free style, yet the rhythm is not lost in meaning; and the meaning in rhythm. There is perfect co-ordination between the two, and the harmony runs through the words and lines like a runnel uninhibited. And the reader can experience it effortlessly. His poetry is neat and tidy in its expression. It is devoid of jagged fragmentariness and inchoate expressiveness. His experiences, sentiments, emotions and feelings are distinctly his own, very much Indian. Raja has undoubtedly proved through his poetry that Indian poetry in English does not suffer from the dearth of talents.

Indian English Poetry was limited in the Pre-Independence days. It was both imitative and derivative. On the contrary, the modern Indian English poets have created enormous output which is neither derivative nor imitative in nature. It is indigenous, very much individualised. It is here, Dr. Raja's poetry is neither imitative nor derivative. His poetry is his own, self-made. It is his personal encounters moulded and shaped in his own inimitable style.

Yet another significant quality of Raja's poetry is that there is no serious obsession on any thing in his poetry. There are no undertones or hidden meanings evoking sensuality, nor can any one find any esoteric meanings. Instead, there is a vibrant humour, seeking freedom from too much intellectualism, imagery and metaphor. His poetry is lucid, objective rhythmically beautiful, and scrupulously honest in its effort to be accurate, non-serious, humorous, satirical and meaningful. If poetry, as Coleridge said, is "rationalised dream", for Raja it is neither intellectually rationalised nor deliberately emotional but calm, plain and smooth sailing and less marked by any richly metaphorical suggestiveness. In poem after poem, the poet articulates in simple and straightforward style his common encounters in a humorous way without recoursing to a distinct frame or patterns to them. The result is that his reflections tend to evoke sympathy and understanding from the readers.

REFERENCES

1. Raja, P. *From Zero To Infinity*, 1987. All India Books, Pondicherry.
2. Raja, P. *To The Lonely Grey Hair*, 1997. Busy Bee Books, Pondicherry.
3. Raja, P. *For Your Ears Only* (A collection of essays), 1997. Busy Bee Books, Pondicherry.

8

Vikram Seth's *Beastly Tales* : Humanising Beasts...Beastising Humans

—*Sanjay Mukherjee*

I

Unlike THE GOLDEN GATE I fear
Here there's no "Acknowledgements",
Nor is anyone the author's dear
For "Dedication" ; and the "Contents"
Like the latter's "Introduction" goes
Line by line in complete prose.
Perhaps Seth thinks it'd disturb
To repeat a self-styled authorial-blurb.
No sonnet sets, no : "Hail Muse"
But again with gusto he regales
The readers through these beastly tales :
Ten narratives; Poetry in perfect use.
So let me cut short and be prosaic
Not defer things further in verbal mosaic.

Though the rhyme-scheme might be familiar to discerning readers let me confess that I have concocted this sonnet simply to make a poetic comparison between two 'poetic' works *i.e. The Golden Gate* and *Beastly Tales* by Seth. It is also an illustration of the powerful grip Seth's "*a splendid tour de force of the transcendence of the mere tour de force*" : *The Golden Gate* [as hailed by *The Sunday Times*, London][1] has on a serious reader. If you think this to be an exaggeration I hope you will pretty much agree with me when I say — without a sonnet this time of course — that all future poetry by Vikram Seth will always be compared with this uniquely awesome masterpiece : *The Golden Gate*, just as all future novels by him will be compared with his equally awesome "purse straining, wrist spraining",[2] and time draining novel : *A Suitable Boy*, though much for the wrong reasons like the fabulous signing-amount he received from the publisher, since surpassed by our very own 'Princess of Prose' — Arundhati Roy.

One has to admit however, that Seth has got the gift of the gab, glued to his tongue; rather, to his pen, or, more likely, to his word processor. Whether he is chasing sonnet after sonnet in the former work just mentioned, or page after page in the latter, Seth is a compulsive story-teller in the Indian traditional mode of the *Kathakar* though any one coming across the sonnets in *The Golden Gate* for the first time would easily be mistaken in assuming those to have originated from a *pucca* Yankee yarn. Therefore, this Indian Yankee cannot only spin stories to entertain readers from 'here and there', he knows how to juggle the narrative techniques as well. So, after the strictures of the 590 sonnets in iambic pentameter set rigidly in a definite rhyme-scheme [neither Shakespearean nor Petrarchan ... Sethian if you like!] and after an anthology called *All You Who Sleep Tonight* which can be described simply as : poemly poems (no pun of the pen intended — in which category we can also slot his earlier two anthologies : *Mappings,* and *The Humble Administrator's Garden*) here is a collection of animal stories called (but of course, how else?) *Beastly Tales* and then, as an afterthought Seth adds : *From Here and There.* Then he draws a line, after which, as if suddenly remembering he adds a post-script : *POEMS.*

Talking of post-scripts, this is one thing running common in all of Seth's works. After each title of his work, he has to clarify that it is a travelogue, or a poem, or a translation of poems, or a novel in verse, or a novel. [Digressing very briefly I might as well mention that one of the earliest literary magazines commemorating India's 50th year of Independence was the

Spring '97 edition of the GRANTA which included a 13-word poem by Vikram Seth called *Sampati* spread over into 14 lines (you guessed it, another sonnet!) and post-scripted : *A Petrarchan Sonnet*] so, from his first work in the early '80s [1983, *From Heaven Lake*] to his latest Seth has been quite traditional in his authorial approach to leave minimum possible vagueness in the readers' expectation. As he tells Tabish Khair, he prefers "a style that supplements the story and does not distract from it."[3] And the most immediate step he takes to stem distraction is by putting indicative/informative style markers that his 'x' work is a Petrarchan sonnet, his 'y' work is a novel in verse and so on and so forth.

II

Now, if you need recovering from the golden dazzles of *The Golden Gate* [though (g)old habits die-hard] try reading these beastly poems. They are — to say the least — different [animal protagonists prancing about instead of the familiar monotony of the humans and their habits]. They are also... 'quite cool'; not in the American sense but quite literally because most of the backdrop [or should I say back-growth] being beshrubbed is quite a shady place to be. Especially, when animalled by our known [tortoise, monkey, crocodile and elephant] and not so known [tragopan, polliwog, trent and coot] members of the zoo-zone.

Considering the limits of my patience with my own paper [and your attention-span which dwindles day by day] I shall limit myself to 4 out of the 10 tales and draw my inferences from them. By the bye, Seth feels it necessary to clarify the "from Here And There" of his title and says that out of the 10 tales, 2 are from India, 2 from China, 2 from Greece, 2 from Ukraine and the last 2 straight from "the Land of Gup." But you are never sure if fables really do have a single origin.

A.K. Ramanujan in his unfinished but immensely scholarly book on oral tales from India mentions :

> ...animal tales tend to be political : about how the powerless, the small, and the cunning sidestep or outwit the powerful. It is not surprising therefore that the

> *Panchatantra*, a book of tales meant to educate princes on the way of the world, should consist mostly of the animal tales.[4]

Seth begins his book exactly on the same lines and his first tale is about how a small, powerless monkey outwits a powerful crocodile and saves his own skin. And Seth's dexterity lies in not allowing ever to let either the story or its rendition slip even slightly out of control. Sample, for example, the following lines where he keeps the couplet rhyme-scheme intact while simultaneously incorporating a dialogue between the crocodile and the monkey :

> They were just halfway across
> When the crocodile said : "Toss
> All those mangoes in the water."
> "But these fruits are all I've brought her."
> "You yourself are gift enough,"
> Said Kuroop in accent gruff.
> "Ah, my friend, that's very gracious."
> "Well, my wife's not so voracious —
> And I'm certain that today
> She won't eat fruit. By the way,
> Tell me what your breast contains.
> Mango nectar fills your veins.
> Does it also fill your heart?"
> Said the monkey with a start :
> "What a very curious question."
> "Well, she might get indigestion
> If it's too rich, I suspect."
> "What?" "Your heart." "My heart?" "Correct."[5]

There's also an interesting characterisation of the wicked and vainglorious Mrs. Crocodile who emotionally blackmails her husband to betray his friend — the monkey — and benefactor of many sackful of mangoes, and trap him for her "anniversary treat." But all's well that ends well and the monkey — as you know — wins in the end and the croc-couple are denied their treat. Pretty simple and straightforward as far as the narrative goes, except for the amusing semantic twist : Mrs. Crocodile who imagines herself to be the uncrowned beauty-queen of the amphibian world and dupes her husband to actually believe it to be so [Ah, true it is that love is blind / Man or beast, we're the same kind.] is the wife of 'Kuroop' the hen-pecked hubby — if you can imagine the amalgamation of these two diverse animals : a croc with the characteristics of a chick.

III

All traditional fables validate the triumph of the Good over the Evil. They depict that virtues like honesty, assiduity and devotion finally wins over falsity, pretension and sycophancy; the shadow fades out in the end and the strength of the substance shines through. But this old rule : 'Virtue was rewarded and vice punished' has become a passé these days. In today's selfish, greedy, cruel and utterly indifferent times it is not at all incongruous to see the good living a poor, unnoticed and unrecognised [and often harassed] life and dying the same death. If times change, should stories remain the same? Seth does not believe in ignoring contemporary ground realities. Remember the old tale of the 'slow-and-steady' tortoise? Well, Seth versifies the same here in the "Hare and the Tortoise." And everything happens as we know : one day the lazy, comfort-loving, boastful hare rebukes the tortoise, who, insulted, challenges the hare to a race; and, while the over-confident hare dozes and dreams, the tortoise wins the race. So far so good. But here comes the twist in the tale. I'm sure you didn't expect the BBC to cover the race? [If Seth can create a self-sufficient animal world, why can't they have their very own "Beastly Broadcast Company"?]. So the media is absolutely flabbergasted. How in the fauna world could the torpedo-footed hare lose to the tortoise? To solve this mystery the press abandons the winner and makes a beeline for the loser whom they discover to be a stunningly attractive female specimen only too eager to pose and selectively expose details about herself. Thus she writes a book on her sensational loss which is immediately a sell-out. While the movie-rights are being snapped up by the Beastlywood producers, the hare laughs all the way to her magnificent new mansion and lives happily ever after with a circle of *chamchas* giggling away the evening in gossips. Thus the end which should have come about in these lines :

After the announcer's gun
Had pronounced that he had won,.
And the cheering of the crowd
Died at last, the tortoise bowed,
Clasped the cup with quiet pride,
And sat down, self-satisfied.[6]

is deferred and differed to these lines :

Thus the hare was pampered rotten
And the tortoise was forgotten.[7]

But its the opening that I shall draw your attention to :

Once or twice upon a time
In the land of Runnyrhyme
Lived a hare both hot and heady
And a tortoise slow and steady.[8]

The message therefore is very clear. 'The slow-and-steady-wins-the-race' paradigm has become so ancient and fossilized that it seems to have worked not 'once' but 'twice upon a time' ago. The new moral then is that talent counts no more; you need the razzle and the dazzle to attract the paparazzi to your windows and your doors. Once they are hooked, your name, bank balance and fame are automatically booked.

Taking about talent, you must have heard our very Indian colloquium : "*Aade waqt pe gadha bhi bapp ban baithta hai*" [when things go bad, even the donkey becomes the boss]. Seth seems to have re-worked this epithet a little in his tale "The Frog And The Nightingale" to make it : when times are bad, even a *maindhak* (frog) becomes a Mozart. Nightingale reminds us of Keats' famous Ode but here she is no source of inspiration except monetary and this tale is the classic case of a male middle-man exploiting a talented but a worldly unwise female. It seems Seth has quite a bit of knowledge in Indian classical music.[9] [A Suitable Boy has a few metaphors from music.][10] This fable is an apt comment on the Indian music scenario and reminds me of an interview I heard on TV of the Sarod maestro Amjad Ali Khan where he says that there is much confusion in the name of Fusion [synthesis of western and Indian notes] going on in Indian classical music these days. As far as popular music is concerned, we have the ubiquitous presence of the blatant copiers, our Maliks and Lahiris of the film-world who never hositate to lift any tune from anywhere so long it is catchy enough to sell. On a larger extent, this verse fable is quite important in this anthology because it's a lament on the degeneration of Art in general in these days of technology driven gimmicks [trick-photography, photomorphing, computer graphics, fusion, remixing and so on]. Tangentially speaking, this poem gives us an idea as to why Seth himself adheres to a certain form(at) in his poetry when all around we find total irreverence to and abandonment of rules giving way to massive experimentation in form and technique in today's poetry. Perhaps Seth conforms to the belief that to innovate and write meaningfully within a framework and rules is the toughest test for an artist. Therefore Seth proves to be quite consistent in the Artist's self-reflexiveness on his art. In *The Golden Gate* he was pre-occupied with iambic tetrameter as a form, in *A Suitable Boy* he muses on the parallel between the Ganga and its tributaries and writing a novel, and here we find him indirectly reflecting on poetry again.

This paper would not be complete without a mention of the final poem, the longest in this anthology and the only one where man makes an appearance — paradoxically — threatening the disappearance of the animals from the face of this earth. It's once again a comic tale, attaining, however, a grotesque dimension in its depiction of the most dangerous specimen of the modern Indian man : the politician. The moral — of a wildlife brutally massacred and an ecology horrendously depleted through senseless industrialisation and abuse of natural resources is chillingly anticipated [but not stated — this is also the only fable out of the ten here not to have an explicit moral] in the following lines :

> For nowhere lies beyond man's reach
> To mar and burn and flood and leach.[11]

And yet, Seth felt he would not like to end on a pessimistic note because that wouldn't gel properly with the otherwise pervasive playful tone of this book. So he takes the middle way out and defers a definite conclusion with the following lines :

And so I'll end the story here.
What is to come is still unclear.
....
I do not know and cannot say;
Indeed, perhaps, I never may.[12]

IV

The category : Children's Stories is quite a misnomer according to experts in Children Literature [henceforth CL] like J.R. Townshend who opines : "Children books are written by adults, and in the main bought by adults. The whole process is carried out at one, two, three or more removes from the ultimate consumer."[13] However, the twentieth century debates on CL primarily define it into two modes. One is in term of genre, that is CL is defined by a set of internal conventions which distinguish it from other genres. [As McDowell argues : "Children's books are generally shorter, they tend to favour and active rather than a passive treatment, with dialogue and incident rather than description and introspection."[13]] Alternatively, CL is seen as a sub-genre of a larger category such as fantasy wherein authorities on CL like Diana Waggoner argues that, "The whole point of fantasy is to establish a credible universe."[13] The second mode defining CL focuses on address; that is, it argues that CL is that which addresses children. [As Aidan Chambers says, "The fact is that some books are clearly for children in a specific sense — they were written by their authors deliberately for children."[13]]

Beastly Tales qualifies as CL on more counts that the two test-modes enumerated above. The sing-song rhyming couplets [Once upon a time a frog/Croaked away in Bingle Bog./Every night from dusk to dawn/He croaked awn and awn and awn.][14] lend themselves so smoothly and easily one into the other that we can set them to our own tunes [no need to be a Bollywood copycat] and transform them into a children's dance-drama. Or, on a more placid note, you can simply read them out as bed-time stories to put your child to sleep. [Who remembers lullabies these days, not to mention being able to sing them out, and that too not like the frog.] The characters in these poems are of such range and variety and so interestingly delineated that this book can be a wealth of ideas to any animation artist who can easily transform them into a comic strip or an animated tele-serial. [In fact the book contains a few hilarious caricatures by the famous cartoonist Ravi Shanker.]

The visual possibilities emanating from the poems in *Beastly Tales* in no way diminish its aurality. In fact long after we have finished the book, the narrator's voice keeps on echoing in our ears : a narrator who is the *universal adult*[15] telling his story to the universal child;[15] because to an adult reader these tales arouse a long slumbering desire for a simple, memorable story. A desire that died with fleeing away of childhood, a desire which in fact reminds us of our own childhood and the tales we had heard once upon a time — from a parent, or a grandparent — and today come to recognise them as part of the rich Indian tradition of oral tales : *The Panchatantra, Betal Pachchisi, The Jataka Tales, The Hitopadesha, Kathasaritsagar* among others; a tradition that is sadly vanishing and is looked down upon as outdated these days. It is interesting to note here that the accounts of creation about the origin of things in *The Puranas* are mostly fictional. So too is the beastly world created in *Beastly Tales*. This immensely recitable Indian tradition of orality — that also has a strong performance orientation — descends from our ancient *akhyanas* and *gathas* [ballads] and *itihas* — puranas [sagas of gods, kings, sages etc.]. Those who attribute Vikram Seth's 'The Golden Gate' to be inspired by Pushkin's *Eugene Onegin* would definitely concede that with *Beastly Tales* Seth shows ample knowledge of the Indian mode of the narrative which, according to the 'radical of presentation' may be distinguished from the lyrical mode. But there are a large number of lyrics in our literary tradition wherein a fairly recognisable narrative thread is woven into lyrical compositions [like lyrics in Surdas' *Sursagar* and Tulsidas' *Kavitavali*]. But Seth reverses the technique in *Beastly Tales* keeping the universal adult — universal child paradigm in mind and thus in a predominant narrative mode, he weaves through a lyrical strain. Hence the Fable — of which the most common is the Beast Fable where animals talk and act like the human types they represent — becomes an easy genre to choose.

Lest you — the rigidly progressive adult group of readers — think too much talk on CL, childhood and the universal child as becoming a wee-bit childish, let me categorically state that *Beastly Tales* is a piece of CL in the same way as *Robinson Crusoe*, or *Gulliver's Travels*, or *Alice in Wonderland*, or *Animal Farm* is. That is, the more we move from the performance level to the textual level, the more multifarious in meaning and serious in nature the discourse becomes. To a serious reader and/or a student of literature, in addition to the satisfaction of getting a good read incorporating a diverse thematic display of enduring relevance [Friendship, Love, Faith, Betrayal, Cunningness, Sycophancy to name a few] there is the amazing vocabulary of Vikram Seth not to mention the easy-flowing assonance and alliteration that goes along with [Deeply *dirked* the dozing king] in spite of sticking to a simple rendition, the unusual — and clever — rhyme-endings [Like an unrepentant bounder/Who allured the pressmen round her; Gibble-gabble all the way/Let her spell "Complete" with K], the subtle allusions [Martin Cardinal Mephisto/And the Coot of Monte Cristo], the witty puns [Mallard and Milady Trent] and the tongue-in-cheek Indianisms ["Oh, Miss Hare, you're so appealing/When you're sweating."].

Fables, like fairy tales are told to hand down to the posterity a message. By their very intrinsic nature, these two genres are the easiest to retain in the collective memory of a society for the longest duration, but are often discarded when they can't keep pace with the times. Vikram Seth, by subverting the moral/message of the fable in the *Beastly Tales* has conformed them to reflect the contemporary reality thereby keeping these delightful narrative pieces in currency for atleast another generation because towards the end of this book it becomes very difficult to determine whether modern man has become more animalistic or modern beast, more humanly.

NOTES AND REFERENCES

1. Rear Jacket of the novel.
2. "Vikram Seth's *A Suitable Boy* : *A Critique*." Avadhesh Kumar Singh, *Critical Practice* : Vol. III, No. 1, Jan. 1996, pp. 79-98.

3. Khair, Tabish. 1993. "Oh Boy". *The Sunday Times* of India Review : Feb. 28, p. 1.

4. Ramanujan, A.K. *A Flowering Tree and other oral tales from India.* 1997, New Delhi : Viking (Penguin India) pp. 217-18.

5. Seth, Vikram. *Beastly Tales From Here And There.* 1992. New Delhi : Viking (Penguin India) pp. 4-5. (Hereafter mentioned as BT.)

6. BT, p. 39.

7. BT, p. 41.

8. BT, p. 33. (italics mine)

9. "What I like most about a *raag* is the *alap.* But obviously no *raag* is complete without the *drut,* the *vilambit.* And in the novel too, when various strands come together, when pieces begin to fall in place, the momentum picks up." (Seth talking about *A Suitable Boy* in an interview with Dileep Padgaonkar in 'The Times of India' : July 27, 1993. p. 7)

10. Amit, a writer in the novel tells Dr. Ila Chattopadhyay and Lata : I've always felt that the performance of a *raag* resembles a novel — or atleast, the kind of novel I'm attempting to write. (394)

11. BT, p. 76.

12. BT, p. 93.

13. All references on CL are from Deepta Achar's article "Adult Talk : on Defining Children's Literature" in *Critical Theory Western and Indian.* Prafulla C. Kar (ed.) 1997, New Delhi : Pencraft International, pp. 180-90.

14. BT, p. 63.

15. I have borrowed these two terms from Birendra Kumar Bhattacharya's article "some thoughts on Narratology" in *Narrative, A Seminar.* Amiya Dev (ed.) 1994, New Delhi : Sahitya Akademi. pp. 30-38.

9

Zen Harmony with Earth and Sky : A Study of Sinha's "Harbour Lights"

—*B.P. Sinha*

Aristotle was the first critic who regarded literature as a re-creation of disjointed fragments of expressions. Dante rightly says "Poetry and the language proper for it are an elaborate and painful toil."

Every great artist re-conquers afresh and adds a new note to the gamut of human perception. He annexes large tracts of human experience to the province of art. Hence there is novelty of his experiments and adventure.

A great critic Abercrombie rightly says that in poetry, the imagination of the poet "escapes from his self-consciousness and becomes the property of the world to make a moment of his experience come to life."

Before me there is a collection of poems written by Dr. Ravi Nandan Sinha. He has been publishing his poems since 1987 internationally. It has been more than a decade that he has maintained continuity which is very essential for any creative artist.

My journey through the poems of Dr. Sinha has been an immensely painful experience of contemporary realism as if crossing a dark tunnel. Suddenly I find myself thrown to an island of despair and gloom but still in the midst of loneliness there is a signal of Harbour Lights.

The river has moved close to my house,
Every night I hear
Its insane whisper

And from the philosophic to mundane — the stark reality, the anguish. The poet attacks the snobbery and intellectual aloofness in the poem *Famine*

The deer have gone away
In search of water,
The secret language of these forests
Is yet to be learnt by those
Who swear by it
Famine is news
Seminars will be organised, speeches made,
old scores settled, political gains calculated,
pain never sold so well.

The poem *Famine* is a hard hitting one at our sensibility. It has becomes a global phenomenon. The marginalised person is speechless.

To a Child in a Bombed City makes us confront with the dark realities of our present existence from the point of view of a child. He has some telling comments to make :

For ever will the scorched womb hold you,
For ever will sad eyes wait for you
To step out into the sun.

The devastating realities in the poems *In a New Country* makes you aware of the frustrating experiences.

Celebrating the festival of faith
Molested in full view of countless
Fathers, brothers, friends and lovers.

These lines remind me of a famous poem *Crossing the Terminus* by Shaileshwar Ghosh, who writes :

I found no life boat for our sinking civilisation
Look, look at our wives and mothers
Bourgeois whores and poor beggars.

The poet himself in the agony of composition perpetuates in his poems an order of existence which is constantly crumbling beneath his touch.

As the last rays of the sun
Steam through leaves
Waiting for death

Imagery of 'virgin white page' and 'shades of blues and greys' from the poem *Seedless* reminds me a few lines from the death poem of William Carlos Williams

If a man die
It is because death
Has first
Possessed his imagination

Despite discussing the hopelessness, the stark confrontations, the poetry of Mr. Sinha is not only thought provoking but musical and sensuous. There is intimate relationship with life. There is natural speed, rhythm and melody; Kahlil Gibran has said in his famous book *The Prophet*.

— Only when you drink from the river of silence shall you indeed sing

These are very prophetic words of Kahlil Gibran.

Our poet makes us aware by returning to the inner consciousness for realisation.

The poem *Our enlightenment* is a very simple poem of Bodhisatva which brings us to a state of emptiness of Nirvana. This poem and the other smaller poems like *Faces, Secret, Dreams* can be compared with Japanese style of poetry — the Haiku style which was greatly influenced by the Zen masters.

A Japanese Zen Haiku poem

Entering the forest
He moves not the grass
Entering the water
He makes not a ripple

How beautifully the Haiku poet says that the full moon entering into the forest moves not even the grass...so silent.

Secret is a master-stroke of Zen style of Haiku where the poet says

> Trees bring heads
> Together in a green whisper
> Sharing secrets.

Dr. Sinha is aware in his nature poems of the fact that the whole existence is dancing, rejoicing, it is drunk completely with blissfulness. He has used the imagery of green whisper in a very sublime and dramatic manner. The poet has used the images very carefully, beautifully and with a golden touch.

Just notice the use of images like-eyeless missile, shades of vulture wings, blues and greys. The sky is stranger, Like your pale fingers, The sun in yellow turban. The image of the sky in abundance, symbolises longingness to know the unknown, the dimensions of space and timelessness. His concerns are primal. The images have cathartic appeal. Slowly the gestalt happens within.

As I said earlier despite the despair and loneliness there is a signal of harbour lights, these mystical lights spiritually transport your awareness to the transcendental consciousness, to the consciousness of Zen where life is in harmony with death; the earth is in harmony with the sky, day is in harmony with the night.

> The breeze whisper old stories
> Remembered and forgotten
> Dusk descends and the earth dreams.

NOTE

Harbour Lights (Anthology of poems) : Ravi Nandan Sinha, Writers Forum, Ranchi.

10

Daruwalla : His Language and Style

—*Birendra Pandey*

During the early sixties a sudden change was discernible in the works of the "new poets". The poets represented startling changes in viewpoints, themes, imagery and the use of the languages. Remarking towards the special traits of these poets, Mr. David Mc Cutchion, a well-known critic of Indo-English, literature says, "The poets of the fifties are fresh, inventive and individual. English is the natural medium of expression...not an alien tongue but the language in which their feelings find from most satisfyingly, the language in which they make love, as Mr. Lal would say".[1] Nissim Ezekiel, Dom Moraes and P. Lal have done yeoman service to the post-Independent Indian poetry in English. Actually, the "new poets" started to work in a hostile atmosphere. Thus, it would not be wrong to say that the new poetry had its birth in the soil of revolt, challenge, modernity and experimentation. This new genre of poetry differ from the old one not only in its subject matter, creative urge and awareness but also in its technique and craftsmanship. Thus, the works of the "new poets" added new dimensions to the Indian poetry in English. They have dealt with the contemporary issues quite realistically using new diction, imagery and rhythm. This change in their attitude generated a genuine concern for technique and craft in the younger poets of the generation. As a result of this, there appeared a host of experimentalists, such as Pritish Nandy, K.N. Daruwalla, Jayanta Mahapatra and Arvind Krishna Malhotra on the landscape of Indian English Poetry. These poets have successfully steered the new poetry to the modernity adding to it fresh meaning and depth commenting on the "new poets". Dr. K.R.S. Iyengar says, "The Western influences are still there : but even more than the 'content' it is the expression and the technique that are being adjusted to the needs of the new age. Hoping Yeats, Eliot, Auden and Dylan Thomas, perhaps even Allen Take and Wallace Stevens have thought our poets the import of taking their art seriously!"[2] Indo-Anglian poetry, Nissim Ezekiel and K.N. Daruwalla are especially notable for consistency and maturity.

The new modernist poets convey their experiences through proper form with a lot of craftsmanship. In their works from and meaning are interdependent, quite contrary to them are the other poets who are primarily concerned in saying a thing, craftsmanship is the secondary issue of them. Dr. A.K. Shrivastava and Dr. Suman Sinha comment on this aspect as follows : "Our other poets considered it more important to be able to say a thing than in the manner of saying it. There was always a tale to tell to a vignette or a landscape to unfold, a metaphysics to expound an emotion to convey and there is in this poetry impressive surancess and precision of the underlying conception ideas message. But the echo-interference of imported models almost always stunted the growth and full maturity of what they wished to convey, and created that may best be described as a disbalance of tension in the poem, the form and content of which pulled in opposite directions, if the former pulled at all. There was to be sure an occasional mighty line a haunting lyric, a well-made sonnet and any number of choice phrases, but the point of special distinction was inevitably the underlying idea.[3] August this background, one finds Nissim Ezekiel to be the first among the neo-modernists who has consistently equally stressed the importance of craftsmanship and the subject matter in a poem. K.N. Daruwalla, R. Parthasarathy, A.K. Ramanujan, Adil Jussawala, Jayant Mahaptra and Shiv K. Kumar are known as the poet of dedication. Their works reveal their great consciousness for craft. In their works one finds them constantly conscious towards content tone, structure and control. To quote Pritish Nandy : "There is a sense of discipline all throughout but this discipline in not a fatuous imitation of English verse-habits and worse. It inculcates an awareness of control as opposed to the orgiastic emotional abandon of the earlier poets like Aurobindo and Sarojini Naidu. In fact, this is the strange thing about recent Indian poetry in English. It is generally controlled and disciplined.[4]

Similarly, one finds the contemporary poets experimenting consciously in the field of imagery. These poets have abandoned the old and conventional models of imagery. They are found inclined towards bald and powerful imagery which is realistic and economical. Though Daruwalla started writing poetry in the late seventies, he has a meteoric rise and he is a poet of great promise. He equals Nissim Ezekiel, Kamla Das and R. Parthasarathy so far poetic contribution is concerned and in some respect such as depth of feeling language economy and originality of sensibility he even appears to be superior to some of his contemporaries. He is a conscious craftsman. In his best poem, theme and tone, structure and imagery interact in creating an absorbing human drama which has few parallels in Indian poetry in English. One finds Daruwalla drawing poetic sustenance from myths, rituals, festivals and religious performances. In 'Mehar Ali, the keeper of the Dead', 'The Parsi Hell', 'Aag Matam', 'Sixth Moharram in Lucknow' and 'The Mazars of Amroha' one finds Daruwalla dealing with the theme related to myths and rituals. Painting to a Tibetan myth which relates that one day the goddess would descend on the earth to take away the dead, he writes in 'Mehar Ali, the keeper of the Dead' :

> Red rain will fall
> as the goddess descends
> her rain-red hair
> streaming backwards in the wind,
> to cart away the dead
> in the folds of her mists.

In similar way, 'Aag Matam' and 'Sixth Moharram in Lucknow' and 'The Mazars of Amroha' refer to the rituals practised by the two sects of Muslims on the eve of Moharram and to a legend respectively. In the opening lines of 'Aag Matam' reforming towards the immortal sacrifice of Hussain and the ritual practised in his pious memory Daruwalla writes :

Alams held aloft the procession comes
(a though bilisters along the ariel skull :
so also shoulder high, the Imam's enemies
carried his severed-head, spiked to a clear)
Alams held aloft, green sciced with stained topaz
the green which the arab soul hungers for
spliced with the brown retalities of the desert
the process emerges from the Imambara.

Similarly in 'Sixth Moharram in Lucknow', he writes :

The breast-beating thyds away, as the
lament rises 'Hai Hussain! Hussain! Hussain!'

Likewise he refers to Hindu-rituals and myths in the poem 'The Water front' such as 'Dassasvamedh' 'Rinddan' mantra 'gayatri' 'Panchtirtha' etc. In 'The Parsi Hell' he has made use of 'Chinvat Bridge', 'gathas' and 'dakhmawell' which are related to the Parsi myth. So it would not be wrong to say that Daruwalla's poetic vision is deeply rooted in myths. His reaction towards the rituals performed by different sects is not pleasant because he feels himself alienated from them.

Daruwalla's poetry has smooth rhythmic flow. The sudden change in rhythms provides breathing gap in his verse. He writes in free verse but his lines mostly have vowel-endings or soft consonant-endings. This brings his verse almost to the rhyming scheme. In the following lines it can be seen how swiftly the rhythm varies but how effectively the poet conveys the gathered up experiences through them :

Pairs of padded feet
are behind me
astride me
infront of me
the footpaths are black feet
converging on the town
brown shoulders black shoulders
shoulders round as orbs
muscles smooth as river-stones glisten
till a dry wind scourges
the sweet form off their backs.

In the above quoted lines one notices rhyming pattern almost near to coherence. Besides they are also notable for beautiful functional images and well-chosen words. Here 'the town' bears the image of a concave mirror and the people that of the rays of light. Likewise 'smooth muscles' bear resemblance with weather-torn well rounded stones.

Daruwalla makes frequent uses of irony and satire to express himself. At some places he makes the situation quite vivid by making the powerful use of irony. As in the underquoted lines, it is found how trenchantly he digs at the medicine men for their lukewarm tendency towards the patients and also for the constant fear of death he lives in :

> the hospital floors are marble-white
> black bodies dirty them
> nurses in white habits
> unicef jeeps with white bonnets
> doctors with white faces receive them.
> Who says they have cholera?
> they are down with diarrhoea
> who says it is cholera?
> it is gastro-enteritis
> who says they have cholera?

A note of deep irony runs through the above lines. The poet gives expression to his simmering anger at the unsympathetic attitude of the medicineman towards the suffering multitude by ironically presenting the situation. He succeeds in having his say without directly projecting himself in the debate. This high degree of objectivity adds greatness to the craftsmanship of Daruwalla. One never finds his person intruding in the affair.

The other great characteristic of Daruwalla as a poet is his power of generalisation. He begins his poem with an individual note but without any great difficulty he makes it universal in character. As in 'Mother' he starts sketching his aged and crippled mother but by his immense power of generalisation, he makes the sketch of his mother of universal nature. This special quality in Daruwalla highly speaks of his craftsmanship :

> Your spine goes creaking now
> across the bow of your body,
> your skin preserves the past in
> its creases.

Likewise referring to his mother's pangs of separation at her widowhood at the fire of everdying love, he says in a generalizing tone :

> I think something shrivelled
> within you, Mother,
> the day you broke your bangles
> and shook the lion-dust
> of my father from your brow

The above lines are remarkable not only for the poet's power of generalization but also speak highly about the economy of word. Here Daruwalla adeptly presents the individual sorrow in universal way by making the use of well-chosen economical words. The same trait of Daruwalla can be also seen in the following lines of 'for my daughter' (Anaheita) :

> You have armlets of beads,
> black and red and topaz
> that brave the dark arrows of the evil eye.
> Brandy in the novel
> drives the cold away
> your novel-cord is the same
> your mother had and her mother
> before her — an elongation in time

A poet's imagery, generally shoots out from his own experience. Consequently it is found that most of the images used in Daruwalla's poems have sprung up from his experience as a police officer. Hence, most of them vivifies violence, destruction and death. Even in the sensuous thing, he finds something ugly offensive and dreadful. By contrasting the objects of his poetic vision with their just opposites, Daruwalla effectively has his say. Referring to the people who carry the dead to the crematorium of the burial, he calls them 'Palanquin-bearers of a different sort' and to the dead being carried by them, he adds, 'on the string-beds they carry no hand-smeared brides.' In short as his poetic tool Daruwalla juxtaposes with the dead and ugly to have the desired effect which is certainly a modernist trait. This technique is visible in the following lines :

> They are palanquin-bearers of a different sort
> on the string-beds they carry
> no henne-smeared brides.
> Prone upon them are frail bodies
> frozen bodies delirious bodies
> some drained of fever and sap
> Some moving others supine
> transfixed under the Sun.

Likewise depicting the ugly and repulsive girls, he writes in "The Epiletic" :

> thin scrawny girls
> carved out of a single thigh
> hysteric quail-like brides
> banging their foreheads on the floor
> and loose-fleshed women with
> a foetus and a demon
> in their ballooned belies.

Quite contrary of Daruwalla, the neo-romanticists are over found to be fed with beautiful and attractive things. Daruwalla, like other new poets expresses his experience through well chosen concrete images. His sensuousness gets expression in the following lines of 'Monologue in the Chambal Valley' :

> Do you recall how it was with the women
> when we started? tant-breasted ones from the hill
> brown ones from Bihar-Soft and overrip
> daughters of the desert/daughters of the forest tribes?

In the following lines, it is again seen how the poet graphically describes the moments of man's sexual excitement and also the process of his being lulled down through the fine images of 'Falcon Fury and the dove' : this is a part of Daruwalla's poetic technique as stated earlier;

> And heal with your own bodies;
> that is the crus of love;
> the falcon-fury of the moment

turns into the dove.
The face as spirit, the fake as flesh
blend in the face as love.

Again it can be seen how the poet describes irresistible physical passion through well chosen concrete images, functional in nature in the following lines :

However you bury the shadow in the heart
under stapes of concrete and coil of bone
however you wall the cave-impulse at the mont,
it will hammer at the sides and break free,
however you bury the shadow in the heart.

Daruwalla has given dramatic touch to some of his poems which have been written in "monologue" or 'soliloquy such as monologue in the Chambal valley', 'Mistress, Requiem for a Hawk' and 'Mehar Ali, the keeper of the Dead,' etc. In 'monologue' Daruwalla has tried to explore the subconscious of man. In monologue in the Chambal valley the poet brings to light the inhuman nature of the bandit chief as well as his contempt for womanhood. Likewise it also exposes the government officials who are hands in gloves with the criminals and antisocial elements. The use of soliloquy and narrative helps the poet in presenting his feelings vividly without himself being a party to it. Due to the adoption of this mode, nowhere the poet is found to be intending in the poem. Besides, like a play the poem has dramatic growth. In the beginning of it we are informed of the content which gradually complicates and reaches the climax and after it, there is sudden anti-climax. In the beginning of the monologue it is given to know how the bandit chief started with the procession. Gradually it comes to be known how he turned into a hardened criminal from a trader in flesh and lastly the revelation of mental restlessness and agony serves as the anti-climax of this poetic drama in miniature.

Similarly 'The Mistress' has a dramatic beginning. The poet presents his mistress *i.e.*, Indian English as a woman of loose morals. He accuses her of ingratiating others as well as him. By presenting his feelings dramatically, he keeps the readers spellbound unless he makes this dramatic revelation that the woman talked about is nobody else but the language he uses.

Daruwalla appears to have consummated in the use of this technique especially in the poem, 'Requiem or a Hawk'. The poem starts with the declaration of an ornithologist that the actual habitat of 'hawk' was at least a hundred miles away from the sea-cost where its fossil was found. This revelation serves as the exposition of the play which is going to be stagged in the poem. The issue further complicates as the geologists carry out investigations as to the correctness of the observation made by an ornithologist. The issue reaches its climax as a tent city has sprung up in the desert scrub and reception are arranged to receive the Sheikh who comes there to celebrate the birth of the bird at its original habitat. The poem reaches its anti-climax as the Sheikh leaves the trained hawks in the air which suddenly fall and meet their sudden death. The tragic death of the hawks is followed by darkness enveloping the earth and shrill. Cry of the crickets, piercing the silence. And after all, the underlying current of irony and satire makes poem a great success.

Like other 'new poets', Daruwalla also, is found consciously experimenting in new imagery. To express, the insatiable thirst for blood of the rioting people, Daruwalla makes use of a new image, not earlier in vogue, in the expression 'barracuda-eyes searching for prey'. Likewise 'that mars of liquefied flesh seething in fear stands for a man living in constant fear of death the marionette head for a senseless man, bled ched white and utterly raped for an unaemie and exhausted person, stalactite becomes symbol of cosmic vitality and energy, 'tonsured heads' for people with completely shaved head 'colour of daggered flesh for redness of melon and 'buzzard-winds' for violent wind and so on so forth. In short, Daruwalla has presented his experience through quite new and realistic images.

Daruwalla's coinage of words is Indian. With a view to giving smooth rhythmic flow to his verse he coins words in Indian fashion, such as blue bottles, mainland, smokestack, treeline, floor-boards, toadstool, dragonfly, chrissake, rucksack, sailboats, etc.

Daruwalla also uses rhyming lines in order to heighten the effect of his poetic work. This also adds to the swift flow of his feelings :

The serpent-waters unwinding from their coils
his inturmoil
down the flagstones, Nothing's bluer,
not at he, not
comet-fires
nor crystal nor sapphire;
no speculum of a mineral-coloured bird
is so intense,
This blue dot is the word.

It is often said that Daruwalla has used journalistic English in his poetry but this is not the whole truth. Excepting a few poems, rest have been written in quite simple and intelligible diction. This adds to the fluency of speech and smooth flow of emotion and sense. In 'Hemanta' he writes :

She who caught her
stealing back at first light,
said, 'there is mustard flower
on your back, be careful,
it is getting to be winter,
you may catch cold.'

In his earlier poetic works, Daruwalla had failed at places in using punctuational marks at places. Owing to this fault, he becomes obscure sometimes. But in his later works, one finds correct use of punctuational marks and no lapses in their use. This fact may be versified in the about quotedliness. In the underquoted lines it can be seen how the poet has failed in inserting punctuational marks at places :

Near the iron
the water-urns are emptied
and the 'Kamer's briesting
with peacock feathers
are flung on the temple-dome'

The first and the fourth lines should have a commas at their end and the fifth a full stop.

In his earlier works such as under Orion and Winter poems, the poet has dealt with the contemporary, themes such as drought, famine, pestilence, communal riot, lovelessness etc. He has used irony and satire as his tools in these poetic works, consequently they are incisive and impressive. While in his later works his bent is rather inward. Hence, their incisiveness and impressiveness are not so great as they are in his earlier works.

On the whole, Daruwalla's technicality and craftsmanship occupy a unique place in the domain of modern Indo-Anglian poetry. He is ranked with only Nissim Ezekiel who is known for the simplicity of diction, controlled rhythm and uninhibited poetry. Being a strict follower of the creative circle dedicated to the cause of Winters workshop he has never drifted back to the old modality and technique of the neo-romanticists. The poet has expressed himself through his works using new idioms, phrases and realistic images. He has not ignored the physical aspect of man in his poetry. On the contrary he has made it all the more sensuous and lively by using apt phrases and well-chosen images. Commenting on Daruwalla, Nissim Ezekiel writes "To most Indo-Anglian poets', simple expression of emotion with a sprinkling of imagery exhaust the craftsmanship. They rarely attempt the dramatic, the creation of characters and situations, the poetic dialogue and the sustained reflection on an experience. Even descriptive skill is rarely demonstrated. Daruwalla is in a different class." At another place while comparatively looking on Daruwalla (he) Ezekiel remarks, "By putting Daruwalla among his contemporaries one sees how he scores heavily over them. By depth of feeling economy of language and originality of insight, Daruwalla commands respect."[6]

REFERENCES

1. S.C. Saha, *Modern Indo-Anglian Love Poetry*, Writers Workshop, Calcutta, 1971, p. 13.
2. K.R.S. Iyengar, *Indian Writing in English*, p. 91.
3. Pritish Nandy, "Indian Poetry in English : The Dynamics of A New Sensibility," *Indian Literature*, Vol. XIV, No. 1, 1971, p. 12.
4. Nissim Ezekiel, *Keki N. Daruwalla.*
5. R.A. Singh, *Daruwalla, Assessment as Poet*, Prakash Book Depot, Bareilly, 1991.
6. R.A. Singh, *The Keeper of the Dead* (A Critical Study), Prakash Book Depot, Bareilly, 1992.

11

The Nature of Conflict in Sri Aurobindo's *Perseus the Deliverer*

—*Vinod Kumar Singh*

I

Sri Aurobindo occupies a unique position in Indian English literature. Primarily a seer and philosopher, he achieves in his writings a unique blending of a highly speculative mind truly staggering in its expanse and profundity and a creative genius that can transform the most abstuse metaphysical concepts and realize their full-blooded enactments within rhetorical frameworks of works of art. The bulk and quality of his poems and plays published in the Birth Centenary Library Series justify his claim that he is a poet of great power and versatility and a critic of life and literature of considerable importance. The plays of Sri Aurobindo in no way stand in isolation from the main current of his poetry. They are, rather, complementary to it and are helpful in the manifestation of his peculiar poetic imagination. Sri Aurobindo's position as a playwright is to some extent similar to that of W.B. Yeats and Rabindranath Tagore, in that they are extensions in a dramatic form his most cherished visions and speculations about the nature and worth of human existence and its final destiny. Sri Aurobindo has to his credit five complete plays and a few unfinished plays : *Perseus the Deliver*, *The Viziers of Bassora*, *Rodogune*, *Vasavadutta*, *Eric*. Four of the complete plays of Sri Aurobindo are comedies. Only *Rodogune* is a tragedy. Of the dramatic fragments, there are *Prince of Edur*, *The Maid in the Mill*, *The House of Brut*, *The Witch of Illni and Others*. The dramatic settings and locales of Sri

Aurobindo's plays vary from play to play. For example, *The Viziers of Bassora* is set in ninth century Iraq. *Rodogune* is set in the Syria of ancient Greek history. *Perseus the Deliverer* is set in the Syria of Greek mythology. The scene of *Eric* is set in ancient Norway. The action of *Vasavadutta* is set in India a century after the Mahabharata war.

Perseus the Deliverer in blank verse is the first full length play of Aurobindo. It was written "somewhere between the end of the nineties and the first years of the following decade."[1] It was written during the Baroda Period, the significant seed-time of his life, and was originally published in serial form in the weekly *Bande Mataram* of Calcutta in 1907. Subsequently, it was revised and included in the collected poems and plays of Sri Aurobindo (1942). The two scenes of the play which were not available in 1942 were later found and incorporated in the text of the first complete edition which was published as a book in 1955. The complete text was published in 1972 in volume 6 of the Sri Aurobindo Birth Centenary Library. The legend of Perseus had a profound fascination for Sri Aurobindo and his brother, Manmohan Ghose. However, when the play began to take shape, Sri Aurobindo realized that the legend would have to be modified to suit the dramatic framework as also to embody the dramatist's personal reading of the legend. In the short preface he writes : "the ancient legend has been divested of its original character of a heroic myth; it is made the nucleus round which there could grow the scenes of a romantic story of human temperament and life-impulses on the Elizabethan model."[2] He further added, "the country in which the action is located is a Syria of romance, not of history...; the town of Cepheus must be looked at as a Greek colony with a blonde Achaean dynasty ruling a Hellenised people who worship an old Mediterranean deity under a Greek name. In a romantic work of imagination of this type these outrages on history do not matter. Time there is more than Einsteinian in its relativity, the creative imagination is its sole disposer and arranger; fantasy reigns sovereign; the names of ancient countries and peoples are brought in only as fringes of a decorative background; and anachronisms romp in wherever they can get an easy admittance, ideas and associations from all climes and epochs mingle; myth, romance and realism make up a single whole."[3]

Thus Sri Aurobindo's attraction to the Greek myth had deeper meaning. He was fascinated by the way various human impulses interplay upon each other to gain ascendency over human personality. He probably intended to explore the larger meaning of this psychic drama which is enacted on the theatre of the human soul of visualize how the trappings of civilization are rent asunder under the force of contending impulses and how deeper spiritual truths have to fight against darker, primitive urges in order to finally emerge and direct the soul's journey through the thick forest of bodily desires and material snares.

Sri Aurobindo drew upon numerous sources, Greek, French and English. Through an act of bold creative freedom, he divested the story of the romantic crusts which it had gathered in the course of its passage through literary history, with a view to retaining the simplicity of the original myth. This not only enhanced the dramatic possibilities of the story but also gave him an opportunity to mould and shape it in accordance with his own design.

Sri Aurobindo's aim in treating this myth was to recast it for across his philosophical ideas. Sri Aurobindo as is well known believed that there is an evolutionary process at work behind the visible phenomenon. Darwin had posited this idea at the physical and biological plane; Sri Aurobindo transformed into the spiritual plane. He believed that the process of cosmic evolution has to pass through various stages. Initially man encounters fear and violence and uncertainty in the physical universe and takes refuge in various kinds of religious systems. As the evolutionary process advances, he experiences the power of love and is led to the ultimate with the help of his own inner light. This final vision of man's victory over the dark and demonic forces of the physical universe as well as his psychic universe emerges at the close of the play when Perseus proclaims :

> Then let the shrine
> That looked out from earth's breast into the sunlight,

Be cleansed of its red memory of blood,
And the dread Form that lived within its precincts
Transfigure into a bright compassionate God
Whose strength shall aid men tossed upon the seas.
Give succour to the shipwrecked mariner.
A noble centre of a people's worship,
To Zeus and great Athene build a temple
Between your sky-topped hills and Ocean's vasts :
Her might shall guard your lives and save your land.
In your human image of her deity
A light of reason and calm celestial force
And a wise tranquil government of life,
Order and beauty and harmonious thoughts
And, ruling the waves of impulse, high-throned will
Incorporate in marble, the carved and white
Ideal of a young uplifted race.
For these are her gifts to those who worship her.[4]

What Perseus exhorts his fellows to do is to rise above the terrestrial and embark on their journey to the celestial where the ever-erring human reason finds its true abode in harmony and beauty. The temple of Zeus and Athene is thus invested with a symbolic meaning. Man's journey to the celestial however is fraught with dangers. Like the Magi, Man's ears are assailed by doubts and defeats. His error-prone ego tries to pull him back making his onward march difficult. He has to pay an enormous price for his spiritual upliftment. And not many are able to pay that price; most turn back, cursing themselves for embarking on the upward journey. Sri Aurobindo has also cautioned against the efforts to transcend the world. It would be a futile attempt. What man should instead do is to transfigure the world to make it fit for the Descent of the Supramental. What is needed for this is that man must turn inward to unravel the secret of nature.

As he himself has said "by conscious effort, humanity must proceed inwards into a knowledge of secret principles of Nature and outward and upward towards a cosmic Being. The salvation of humanity henceforth lies not in transcending the world but in transfiguring it so as to make the universe fit for the Descent of the Supra-mental."[5] Organised religions which prescribe various kinds of rituals in order to propitiate various duties so that they are pleased to vouchsafe the boon of bliss only succeed in misleading the people. After all paradise is within us and the best abode of the Divine is the pure and simple heart of man. Andromeda echoes this truth when she tells Perseus —

Let the dire cult
For ever cease and victims bleed no more
On its dark altar. Instead Athene's name
Spread over all the land and in men's hearts.
Then shall a calm and mighty will prevail
And broader minds and kindlier manners reign
And men grow human, mild and merciful.[6]

II

Perseus the Deliverer composed at a time when Sri Aurobindo was in the thick of the freedom struggle in the early years of the twentieth century contained in an embryonic form the quintessence of his vision of true freedom. *Perseus the Deliverer* has a classical structure. Like Marlowe's *Doctor Faustus*, it opens with a prologue in which the central conflict of the play is revealed. On the one hand is Pallas Athene, a friend of man, willing to lend him a helping hand in his spiritual evolution. On the other hand is Poseidon who is determined to obstruct the upward ascent of man. Athene as the goddess of wisdom is opposed to Poseidon's mechinations. Poseidon represents human intelligence which is always engrossed in material considerations. While Athene is encouraging man to rise to Godhead, Poseidon wants to keep man tied down to meaningless rituals and empty observances. Athene says :

Me the Omnipotent
Made from His being to lead and discipline
The immortal spirit of man, till it attain
To order and magnificent mastery
Of all his outward world.[7]

Poseidon remains unmoved and his determination to suppress the growing stature of man remains unruffled. He considers himself to be the custodian of the balance between the divine and the human. He almost accuses Athene of undermining the existing balance by allowing man to outstep his power and usurp what has traditionally belonged to the gods. Poseidon represents the ancient Greek wisdom that gods could demand anything from humans, even their blood. Athene reminds him that he must change his attitude towards man and recognise his right to live his life and seek salvation in the ways he thinks most conducive. Thus the theme of the play seems to be one of conflict between the old anthropomorphic culture of the primitive Greeks which constrained man to respect limits and the new culture of growing scepticism, which though still respecting the traditional value-systems, yet wanted more room for man's instinctive urges and reliance on his moral sense. Poseidon thinks that if the new waves of questioning and scenticism are not checked, anarchy and chaos will prevail. Himself a god of the seven seas which remain untrodden by man, he would like to keep his dominion safe. He is a believer in the iron law; he is untouched by mercy or sympathy when it comes to maintain his tradition-sanctioned authority. In fact he quotes tradition to support his authoritarianism and tyranny. For him the end justifies the means. He leaves no one is doubt when he asserts :

> I am not of the mild and later gods,
> But of that elder world; Lemuria
> And old Atlantis raised me crimson alters,
> And my huge nostrils keep that scent of blood
> For which they Quiver. Return into thy heavens,
> Pallas Athene, I into my deep.[8]

The conflict between Poseidon and Pallas Athene seems to be unresolvable. As custodians of divinity they would avoid a direct clash between themselves. Therefore, they decide to have a proxy war. Both have their non-divine champions. Poseidon is represented by the sea-monster polydaon and Athene is represented by Perseus who is the leader of mankind and represents not only the human urge to master the elements but also the iron will to achieve it. Poseidon clearly understands the odds arrayed against him and man and this only adds to his resolve to take on the forces inimical to man. He declares :

> This is no hour to speak or plan, but to act,
> A presence sits within my heart that sees
> Each moment's need and finds the road to meet it.
> Dread nothing; I am here to help and save.[9]

Further he says —

> My grip is firm on Herpe,
> Athene's aegis guards my wrist; herself
> The strong, omnipotent and tranquil goddess
> Governs my motions with her awful will.
> Have trust in me. Born on my bright-winged sandals
> Invisibly I will attend your course
> On the light breezes.[10]

By declaring that divine blood flows in his veins he underlines the truth that man, though inhabiting the earth has his own divinity of which no one can deprive him. At another place in the play he says —

> Syrians, I am Perseus,
> The mighty son of Zeus and Danae.
> The blood of gods is in my veins, the strength
> Of gods is in my arm : Athene helps me.
> Behold her aegis, which If I uncover
> Will blind you with its lightnings; and this sword
> Is Herpe, which can pierce the earth and Hades.
> What I have done, is by Athene's strength.
> Borne from Seriphos through pellucid air
> Upon these winged shoes, in the far west
> I have traversed unknown lands and nameless continents
> And seas where never came the plash of human oars.[11]

Aurobindo has hinted at the divinity in Perseus at the very outset when one of the characters speaks of Perseus as having all the attributes of gods :

> Perseus, the Olympian's son,
> Whom Danae in her strong brazen tower,
> Acrisius' daughter, bore, by heavenly gold
> Lapped into slumber : for of that shining rain
> He is the beautiful offspring.[12]

Viewed in the context of Aurobindo's philosophical system, Perseus is clearly the symbol of the spirit that has come down to the earth to illumine and invigorate it and to awaken the dormant forces which might accelerate the upward evolution of the matter-bound world. Aurobindo posited his belief in the process of evolution that continues uninterrupted in the universe but he freed it from Darwin's theory of natural selection and the survival of the fittest by transforming it from the biological evolution of the species to the spiritual evolution of the sentient beings. This kind of spiritual evolution is not suigeneris but awaits the descent of the spirit on the earth. Once this Descent takes place, the sentient beings start moving in the direction of order and harmony from gross material preoccupation. From matter which keeps us tied down to our base desires and passion, we move upward, and passing through the two intermediary states we are transformed into the cosmic consciousness. The state of cosmic consciousness may be liked to the realization of what the Vedantins have called the moment of "Aham Brahmasmi." But while in Vedant this realization is analogous to a sudden occurrence without any premeditation, in the system of Sri Aurobindo, it comes at the end, as the final fruit of *sadhana*. To quote Sri Aurobindo :

> Life is the first step of a release of consciousness involved originally, in Matter; Mind is the second step. Evolution does not finish with Mind. It awaits a release into a consciousness which is spiritual and supernatural. The next step in evolution is the development of super Mind and spirit in conscious Being. This cannot be done at once and many preliminary steps have to be taken. Many intervening stages are indispensable in the process of Sadhana (self-discipline) bringing about the ultimate result — an emergence into what has been called the Cosmic Consciousness.[13]

Thus Perseus represents the Supermind and that is why he finds himself in conflict with the votaries of Matter who oppose him and try to stall his efforts of transforming Matter into something greater and nobler. The people of Syria have pledged their faith into the priest but the priest himself remains clogged to Matter. He is indifferent even to Andromeda who represents the higher stage of the life of Mind. Thus Perseus is thrice removed from the people of Syria. Poseidon and Pallas Athene represent the two poles of the whole evolutionary drama — Matter and the cosmic consciousness.

Significantly the most clamorous opposition to Perseus's plans comes from Poseidon who rules over the sea. Symbolically he is even worse than average Syrians and their priests because they are human beings. Poseidon is ironically a god, supposedly closer to divinity who should spontaneously heed the call of Perseus. But he is stubborn and egoistical, interested in preserving his superiority by treating human beings only as objects of torture, degradation and sacrifice. His altar is crimson and his nostrils forever quiver for the scent of human blood. He sows the seeds of disunity and discard among human beings so that they would always turn to him for succour and justice. He is demonic in every sense and a declared enemy of mankind. As the embodiment of evil his power cannot be ignored. Perseus is utterly confused about the true identity of Poseidon for whom he is a foil :

> O thou grim calmness imaged like a man
> That frown'st above the altar : fire Poseidon!
> Art thou that god indeed who smooths the sea
> With one finger, and when it is thy will,
> Rufflest the oceans with thy casual breathing?
> Art thou not rather, lord, some murderous
> And red imagination of this people,
> The shadow of a soul that dreamed of blood
> And took this dimness? If thou art Poseidon,
> The son of Cronos, I am Cronos' grandchild,
> Perseus, and in my soul Athene moves
> With lightnings.[14]

Thus blessed by Athene Perseus takes upon himself the task of delivering mankind from the demonic traps of Poseidon. He is a saviour and a messiah who must ensure not only the physical safety of his followers but also the safety of their souls. There is nothing selfish in his endeavours. Whatever he does is for the good of the whole community who were groaning under the cruel religion of blood-loving Poseidon. Perseus is out to unmask the deity who is vindictive and malignant and by so doing he brings a more humane order of things.

Andromeda also has a symbolic role because she is in complete agreement with the ideals pursued by Perseus. She stands for compassion, grace and kindliness. This aspect of her character comes out when she explains to Perissus the reason for releasing the trapped merchants. She has the capacity to empathise with other experiences :

> Because I would not have their human hearts
> Mercilessly uprooted for the bloody
> Monster you worship as a god! because
> I am capable of pain and so can feel
> The pain of others! For which if you I love
> Must kill me, do it. I alone am guilty.[15]

She is defiant and fearless and is not oppressed by the thoughts of consequences that would follow from her actions. She follows the dictates of her heart. She is not afraid even of eternal damnation provided her action has brought an end to undeserved suffering of somebody even if that suffering has been inflicted by some cruel supernatural agency. She loves mankind and is prepared to go to any extent to help them without repentance or remorse. Andromeda seems to have attained to the highest perfections of what Aurobindo has called the Adhyatma Yoga when the *sadhaka* sees the manifestation of godliness in every tiny creature of the universe. Nothing in this state exists except God. Once a person reaches this state he or she has no personal or self-centred desires. All actions are directed to bringing about peace and joy to all. Even when Andromeda is warned by Pallas Athene she remains unruffled in her mission because she has fully identified herself with the Goddess. Athene says to Andromeda :

> To thee alone I gave
> This knowledge. O virgin, O Andromeda,
> It reached thee through that large and noble heart
> Of woman beating in a little child,
> But dost thou know that thy reward shall be
> Betrayal and fierce hatred? God and man

Shall league in wrath to kill and torture thee
Mid dire revilings.

** ** **

Thou fear's not then? They will expose thee, child,
To slaughter by the monsters of the deep
Who shall come forth to tear thy limbs.[16]

Andromeda however wants only one assurance of the unimpeded love of Athene :

Wilt thou love me?[17]

Pallas Athene gives a prompt positive reply. She assures Andromeda that she would forever abide with her, though remaining invisible. Pallas Athene herself is the symbol of Divine Power. When Diomede visits Andromeda she is dazzled by the lustrous light that forms a hallow around Andromeda's face. Andromeda has finally entered the sphere of *shakti* because Athene has adopted her as her own. Andromeda's surrender has won for her the Divine Grace.

Seen in the symbolic framework of philosophical ideas, specially those of Sri Aurobindo's own system, it is obvious that the nature of conflict in *Perseus the Deliverer*, though apparently between different persons is in essence cosmic. The conflict is between the dark forces of unevolved consciousness where human beings are no better than a carnivorous animals and the forces of grace and divinity through man is transformed into the godhood. The play presents the eternal conflict between evil and good. It is the dramatic version of the *devasur sangram*. At the divine level this is represented by Poseidon and Athene, the former representing the gross, unevolved matter and Pallas Athene, the highest form of Consciousness where discord and disharmony are entirely absent. The same *conflict* is enacted on the human level between Andromeda and Polydaon. Polydaon is ironically a priest but the shrine which is in his charge is a dark one where mercy and kindliness carry no meaning. Thus it may also be the conflict between a religion which has been reduced to rituals and a faith which is simple, straight-forward and unostentations. Andromeda represents the aspiring human spirit which is forever searching for its celestial roots. She aspires for the sun-god and this aspiration symbolizes the jeeva's eternal hankering for the primordial Brahman. Perseus comes in the life of Andromeda as one who would remove the hurdles in her way. In fact, both Andromeda and Perseus aid each other's spiritual evolution.

Thus, in spite of the rush and riot of action which remind one an Elizabethan or Jacobean tragedy, *Perseus the Deliverer* is invested with a spiritual meaning. It is true that while the play was being composed Sri Aurobindo was still in the formative phase of his metaphysical inquiry about the ascent of the human spirit to the forbidding heights of the Cosmic Consciousness. The play gives the first authentic hints of the direction in which the future seer's mind was moving. Concluding we may quote Sri Aurobindo himself :

> For here the stage is the human mind of all times : the subject is an incident in its passage from a semi-primitive temperament surviving in a fairly advanced outward civilization to a brighter intellectualism and humanism never quite safe against the resurgence of the dark or violent life-forces which are always there subdued or subordinated or somnolent in the make-up of civilized man — and the first promptings of the deeper and higher psychic and spiritual being which it is his ultimate destiny to become.[18]

REFERENCES

1. *Collected Poems and Plays*, Vol. 1, p. iii (1942).
2. Sri Aurobindo, *Perseus the Deliverer* (1955), p. 1.
3. *Ibid.*, pp. 1-2.
4. *Ibid.*, p. 145.
5. Quoted by C.P. Ramaswamy Aiyer in Biographical Vistas, p. 266. *Sri Aurobindo's Perseus the Deliverer* by Ashok Mahashabde, *Mother India*, Vol. XLVII, July 1994, No. 7.
6. Sri Aurobindo, *Perseus the Deliverer*, p. 145.
7. *Ibid.*, p. 6.
8. *Ibid.*, pp. 8-9.

9. *Ibid.*, p. 92.
10. *Ibid.*, pp. 92-93.
11. *Ibid.*, pp. 125-26.
12. *Ibid.*, p. 9.
13. Quoted by C.P. Ramaswamy Aiyer in Biographical Vistas, Asia Publishing House, Bombay, 1968, pp. 267-68.
14. Sri Aurobindo, *Perseus the Deliverer*, p. 62.
15. *Ibid.*, p. 80.
16. *Ibid.*, pp. 58-59.
17. *Ibid.*, p. 59.
18. *Ibid.*, p. 2.

12

The Spiritual Progress in the Poetry of T. Vasudeva Reddy

—T. Raghavan

The achievement of T. Vasudeva Reddy as an Indian poet in English has been widely acclaimed by critics in India and abroad. As a farmer-poet hailing from a tiny village of Andhra Pradesh, he has been able to make a distinct contribution to the Indo-English literature. His ability to give uninhibited expression to his experiences in rural India, revealing a voice that is both personal and universal, distinguished him from his fellow-poets.

The sincerity and authenticity of Vasudeva Reddy's poetic utterances have apparently been enhanced in a large measure by his aversion to all sorts of distancing and depersonalizing devices. A deliberate decision on his part to steer clear of all such devices is suggested by some of his poems. He says :

> I shall be myself
> without any dissembling (BR, p. 16)

> with my feet
> rooted to the earth
> I wish to go with you (BR, p. 26)

> Could I run from myself
> No..... (FB, p. 7)

The poet's decision in this regard seems to have resulted from a wholesome awareness of his own innate instincts. Besides, he must also have been alive to the relative lack of true sincerity in some of his distinguished predecessors including William Wordsworth. But the poetic method favoured by him has perhaps undermined the efficiency of the tranquilizing process that should normally precede the making of poetry out of raw and intense emotions in accordance with a Wordsworthian definition of it. The method, however, beings him close to the other definition of poetry as "spontaneous overflow of powerful feelings", by Wordsworth himself.

Vasudeva Reddy's poetry has been aptly described as an "outburst of emotion."[1] The emotional astringency associated with it justifies the replacement of the term "overflow" by "outburst" in its description. Presumably, the poet has no relish for the refrigeration of genuine emotions in the presence of making poetry. His endeavour obviously is to present them as they are without diluting their intensity by any means.

Having opted for the role of a critic of the society of his time, the adoption of a cold-blooded strategy, consistent with the Wordsworthian notions, was a luxury he could hardly afford. For, as is widely realized, the Wordsworthian strategy was essentially a mask, shorn of its trappings, and had rendered the poet's integrity suspect. Vasudeva Reddy believes :

> Polich teaches dissembling
> While sparks of truth slip
> from his drunken lips. (BR, p. 12)

His distrust of rhetorics mentioned by A. Rassell[2] must have been presented by his determination to be for thought in his expression.

Consequently, when Vasudeva Reddy deals with subjects that are close to his heart, the reader is exposed to the heat of his emotions perhaps to an excessive degree. "On the Death of Mrs. Indira Gandhi" (FB, p. 32), "In Memorium" (MM, p. 30) and "In Exile" (FB, p. 28) may testify to that fact. Again, when the so-called leading lights of his day are ridiculed in several other poems, we are often dumb-founded :

> their panchayat is a crafty cobweb
> pregnant with potent poison (BR, p. 11)

the shallow slogans
of our elected leaders
grieve the ruins (BR, p. 30)

while masses groan under his vain promises
his relatives revel in ill-gotten wealth;
The elected leader leads his caste
the self-styled saviour saves his kindred; (FB, p. 33)

For democracy he seems to be the head
while his henchmen sever many a head
he wins by spreading the pall of dread
and slices of momentary bread. (MM, p. 11)

Such poems, evocative as they are of the well-known satires of the Augustan Age, are bound to the significant mainly as records of typical Indian experiences. Of course, they also bear testimony to exemplary courage on the part of the poet.

Prof. K. Venkatachari has thrown a flood of light on the satiric vision of Vasudeva Reddy. He points out how the latter's satires traverse from the general to the particular and rise to the universal.[3]

D.R. Kaltovish has commended the incomparable fusion of biting satire and poetics in Vasudeva Reddy's poetry.[4] What distinguishes his satires from the words of better known poets of his time is the deep humanistic concern in which they are embedded.

Prof. David Kerr has drawn attention to the sociological consciousness and earnest concern for the weal of the society revealed in his poetry.[5] Rosemary C. Wilkinson has observed how his subjectivism soars to the higher level of universality.[6] Prof. Y.P. Singh has also highlighted the universality of his poetry.[7] If T.S. Eliot could place W.B. Yeats on a high pedestal in view of the deeper and more substantial impersonality, that borders on universality, found in his later poetry,[8] one should not grudge allowing a place of honour to Vasudeva Reddy in the galaxy of Indo-English poets.

All the same, one cannot help thinking that such satires, surcharged as they are with noble sentiments, often tend to be rather suffocating, notwithstanding the sardonic humour produced by them. The musical quality of his verse that has earned him high praise[9] does little to relieve that suffocation. The impression at times is of a relative lack of intellectual control over the emotions expressed.

When emotions are thus allowed to gain the upper hand in poetry, the situation that arises may seem analogous to the one that prevailed in the early years of the twentieth century. We are aware how the modernists, led by T.S. Eliot, responded to it, and sought to idealize John Donne, whose poetic technique provided for both thought and emotion going hand-in-hand in poetry. But Eliot himself apparently modified his stance in this regard when he praised the forthright and uninhibited style of the later Yeats although it obviously lacked adequate cerebral control.

The social reformer in Vasudeva Reddy has perhaps sapped his artistic virtuosity at times. If some of us are inclined to brush aside his satiric verse on that score, we should not lose sight of its intrinsic significance and social commitment.

Mercifully enough, a good number of poems of other kinds, too, are found in Vasudeva Reddy's collections. And some of them reveal his capacity for sensitive, imaginative and insightful perception of nature as well as human nature. They also throw hints of a salutary progress in the course of his poetic life.

The poetry of Vasudeva Reddy published so far, has come in four collections : *When Grief Rains*, *The Broken Rhythms*, *The Fleeting Bubbles*, and *Melting Melodies*. Significantly enough, his poetic life has its beginning when grief rains and has led him to melting melodies. R.S. Sudarshanam has found a transition of mood in his poetry from futility to anger, from anger to calmness, and from calmness to prayerful acceptance. He considers it typical of an Indian experience.[10] What is achieved in the process seems to be a spiritual progress which is perhaps universal rather than Indian. Such a development has, in fact, been characteristic of the lives of some illustrious figures of the world literatures including T.S. Eliot. A closer look at the corpus of Vasudeva Reddy's poetry, published hitherto, with a view to determining the possible influences that helped bring about a welcome transformation in his poetry, is bound to be interesting and rewarding.

Vasudeva Reddy's poetry began on a dreary and dismal note in its early phase :

> Jilted by crafty clouds
> the sun-burnt crop looked
> like a dissected corpse
> on the post-mortem table. (WGR, p. 28)

> Life is an endless desert
> full of sands and storms, no oases. (WGR, p. 14)

> A flutter of wings :_
> the sky squawked in requie (WGR, p. 15)

> The nothingness around me gapes and gasps;
> It hardly breathes — baneful breeze : (WGR, p. 24)

The mood of deep depression projected through these lines reminds us of the Hardyan predicament characterized by utter lack of faith in the divine dispensation of justice. And presumably, the post-mortem table portrayed here ones a little to the celebrated image of a patient etherized upon a table in T.S. Eliot's "Love Song of J. Alfred Prufrock."[11] Yet we cannot rule out the possibility of these images symbolizing the poet's own inner landscape. And it may be less than fair to assume that the emotions expressed here are either false or exaggerated. Such an assumption is bound to be insinuating as it suggests a kinship between the poet and the Decadents of the nineteenth century. But the degree of intensity and integrity revealed in the poetry of Vasudeva Reddy may absolve him of the charge of falsity or exaggeration. Moreover, the poet's confession —

> Still some where in me
> A dim desire creeps
> to possess the instinctive mackintosh. (WGR, p. 25)

speak of a complexity that runs counter to the deleterious tendency to allow himself to be submerged by debilitating emotions. Again, when darkness invades his desolate spirit and saps his sinking soul, we are assured —

> Yonder the glow-worm drifts in the dark.
> (WGR, p. 27)

One might presume that the macabre quality of the image in T.S. Eliot's love-song resulted as much from a deliberate attempt on his part to deromanticize poetry as from the feebleness of his own faith. But the situation in which Vasudeva Reddy presented the image did not seem to have warranted a deliberate bid of that kind. His primary concern must have been to be true to himself and to the landscape portrayed. The fact that he has chosen to present such a dreadful picture in isolation may be suggestive of the absence of a comprehensive vision in him at that point of time.

The lack of a vision of the kind in the poet is suggested when he says :

> The earth is round,
> Like a pointless top it revolves. (WGR, p. 22)
>
> I am alone, a forsaken man
> a lone man with a desperate will
> to drift the rudderless course
> to safe shores.... (F.B., p. 9)
>
> Still I steer rudderless
> Gazing at the faint star
> Vainly hoping to come ashore (F.B., p. 16)

The gazing at the faint star may symbolize a desire in the poet to have a strong and assuring faith. Such a faith might well have provided a point to the pointless top and a rudder to his rudderless course. The faintness of that faith, as it exists in him at the moment, is also hinted at by the line. Similar sentiments, projected earlier by Thomas Hardy in a comparable situation, keep reverberating in his poetry time and again :

> You have sustained the life of the Lord
> — who does not redeem you.
> Find your own saviour...... (WGR, p. 16)
>
> While holy harmony rests in cemetery,
> heads of sweat boil on stone walls
> Still the Maker is quiet in the grave. (WGR, p. 32)

What distinguishes the poet from Thomas Hardy is his tendency to keep oscillating between faith and doubt. A poem that records an awakening on his part, for instance, is soon followed by another portraying his lack of faith;

> The mystic "Om" filled the torpid mind
> And heart, seized all the senses
> Entered flesh and blood and every nerve.
> (WGR, p. 40)
>
> The exit of the gasping breath alone
> shall release me from the lingering pain.
> (WGR, p. 41)

We may remember how Hardy remained relatively firm in his lack of faith throughout and revealed an adamantine character unlike him.

We have reason to believe that a feeble faith remained with Vasudeva Reddy even in his early phase. In fact, he was painfully aware of its inadequacy :

> Around a pinch of faith,
> an army of dark bodies
> roll in waves of countless doubts; (WGR, p. 26)

It is quite some time before his faith begins to assert itself. An unambiguous references to it is found only at the end of his third collection of poems :

> I hear the breath of an unseen force
> Formidable and inscrutable in nature
> In the midst of deep mystery around me
> I feel the grace of the Supreme Being. (FB, p. 39)

It is perhaps natural that the collection of poems that follows is *Melting Melodies*.

Man's vision, we are told, can redeem the world filling it with mystery, meaning and human gratitude for existence.[12] It is a deep faith in God that promotes one's capacity for such a vision. And we may safely presume that the relative lack of it in Vasudeva Reddy in his early phase has been largely responsible for the sombre features of the poetry he had written during that phase. Indeed it is a thing for which he had yearned for long.

In the new phase, things which were dull and drab earlier gain a new animation :

> Every piece of ruin, a marvel of art in stone,
> carves a mute message, echoes a faded epic
> each tiny speck an iridescent luminous spark.
>
> (MM, p. 5)

The poet himself becomes aware of the transformation brought about by his new, invigorated faith soon enough, as he starts singing in praise of God in an exhilerated tone :

> Those that believe me
> bathe in the Manasa lake
> and tread the celestial land
> spread with gold dust,
> the rest know no rest
> and end up in the dust. (MM, p. 44)

> Thy unseen presence is now my strength
> to sail and strive, thrive and not to fall. (MM, p. 42)

In the absence of an abiding faith to light up his world and sustain his spirits, the poet was able to draw comfort from his earthly relationships :

> Don't quit my love
> without you
> why should I be here
> and lose my identity
> in the prison of a world (FB, p. 13)

We may recall how Matthew Arnold had tried to impress on his wife long ago the need of being true to each other, as there was nothing worthy of their trust in the world. What is evidenced in the earlier poetry of Vasudeva Reddy is a problem of far greater gravity. In as much as the values of life have been eclipsed almost irretrievably in the new context.

While Vasudeva Reddy's wide humanity and sympathy have stood him in good stead in all sorts of weathers, his keenness and sensitivity have made him alive to the presence of an all-embracing power that is capable of animating not only the world of nature but also the world of poetry. We find his humanistic and altruistic concerns also gaining a new verve and vigour in the wake of his new convictions as he prays to the Lord of the Sacred Hills :

> Fall our hearts will selfless love
> Sow in our lives seeds of light. (MM, p. 43)

REFERENCES

1. David Kerr, Foreword to *Melting Melodies*.
2. Review of *The Broken Rhythms in Poetry Time*, Spring, 1988, p. 100.
3. K. Venkatachari, "Satire in T.V. Reddy's Poetry", *Poetcrit*, January, 1977, pp. 21-28.
4. E.R. Kaltovich, Preface to *The Broken Rhythms*.
5. David Kerr, *op. cit.*
6. "When Grief Rains — A Perspective", *Poetcrit*, Jan. 1990, p. 19.
7. Y.P. Singh, "The Universality of T.V. Reddy's Poetry", *Triveni*, Volume 63, April-June, 1994, pp. 34-37.
8. T.S. Eliot, "Yeats," *On Poetry and Poets*, London : Faber and Faber Ltd., 1957, pp. 257-58.
9. Y.P. Singh compares him with Sarojini Naidu on that score.
10. R.S. Sudarshanam, "T.V. Reddy : A Poet of Choiceless Awareness," *Indian Scholar*, Vol. XV, Jan. 93, No. 1, p. 48.
11. T.S. Eliot, *Selected Poems*, London : Faber and Faber, 1954, pp. 11-16.
12. David Holbrook, *Lost Bearings in English Poetry*, London : Vision Press Limited, Vision Critical Studies, 1977, p. 88.

13

Existentialism in the Poetry of O.P. Bhatnagar

—Kumari Vibha Agrawal

O.P. Bhatnagar has emerged as a major Indian English poet of our era. He is a powerful voice trying to mould the conscience of man for a better world order. His poetry is not bogged down in dreamy romanticism. He has made it stand on the firm ground of existential realism. Bhatnagar is a multifaceted genius. He is a poet, critic, and an anthologist. He is a strong humanist committed to the cause of the poor and the downtrodden. His aim is to uplift them from the mud and mire of their miserable existence. As an artist Bhatnagar shows simplicity in his writings. His poetry sounds the clarion call of revolt against many-faceted oppressions, injustice, corruption, inequalities, moral degenerations and atrocities of man upon man. He is aggrieved to see that in the modern age virtue is over-ruled by vice. He fearlessly and emphatically presents his viewpoint and adroitly portrays how common man has lost his identity in modern times and how he has fallen victim to the hydra-headed evils of society and politics. Among many other characteristic of Bhatnagar's poetry, one great quality is that it breathes the spirit of existential philosophy.

Existentialism in modern literature means the study of basic problem of self. The term existentialism means "pertaining to existence or in logic predicating existence. Philosophically, it now applies to a vision of the condition and existence of man, his place and function in the world and his relation or lack of one with God".[1] It is generally agreed that existentialism derives from the thinking of Soren Kierkegaard (1813-55) expressed specially in his book, *Fear and Trembling* (1843), *The Concept of Dread* (1844) and *Sickness Unto Death* (1848). In these books he elaborates on the belief that man, through his faith in God, can find freedom from tension and discontent. He became the pioneer of modern Christian existentialism. The German philosophers Heiddegger and Jasper expanded this thought and influenced a large number of European philosophers such as Berdyev, Unamuno etc. in whose works were to be found the sources of aesthetic existentialism.

The argument of aesthetic existentialists is that existence precedes essence for it is believed that "Man fashions his own existence and only exists by so doing and in that process, and by the choice of what he does, or does not do, gives essence to that existence."[2] Jean Paul Sartre, the high priest of modern existentialism, presents his interpretations through his novels, plays and philosophical writings and influenced the thinkers world over. Elaborating on Sartre's theory Cuddon says : "In Sartre's vision man is born into a kind of void (*neiaant*), a mud (levisqueux). He has the liberty to remain in this mud and thus lead a passive, supine acquiescent existence (like Oblomov and Samuel Beckett's sad tatterdemalions), in a state in which he is scarcely aware of himself conceivably, experience 'angoisse' (a species of metaphysical and moral anguish). If so, then he would have sense of the absurdity of his predicament and suffer despair. The energy deriving this awareness would enable him to drag himself out of this mud and begin to exist. By exercising this power of choice he can give meaning to existence and the universe."[3]

Sartre further expresses the belief that man can emerge from this passive condition and by an act of will can become committed to social and political life. Through commitment man can make his existence meaningful. Besides Sartre, some of the chief exponents of existentialism have been Simon de Beauvoir, Merleau Ponty, and Jean Whal. The main exponent of Christian existentialism was Gabriel Marcel, the dramatist and philosopher who has written some brilliant critical analyses of Sartre's point of view.

Bhatnagar appears to have been deeply influenced by existentialism. It has always been the attempt of man to realize his identity in the ever growing complexity of life. In poem after poem, he attempts to diagnose the predicament of man in the matrix of existence and fix the poet's role in revealing and mitigating human suffering. Though he does not attempt a scientific and philosophical definition of existentialism, his intuitive insight offers him a clue to the mystery of human existence. Being deeply influenced by the French existential writers such as Sartre and Camus, he finds this philosophy "most suited and valuable of all thoughts for Indian conditions today."[4]

Bhatnagar asserts that he is not influenced by any school of thought of philosophy, his poetry reveals his commitment to the existential line of thinking. He says, "Poetry must explore man, his sufferings, conflicts, and predicaments, hopes, dreams and joys more than the possibilities of his commitments to ideologies, doctrines, redemption and salvation."[5]

For Bhatnagar, search for true self beyond self is futile. The exploration of the self is the key to the theory of existentialism. Heiddegger defines existentialism "as freedom from final commitment unto death." For Sartre, with his negative view, "It is rather a freedom from any such commitment save to the principle of having no commitment at all."[6] Bhatnagar also deals with this issue in his poetry. Bondage restricts man but provides safety; freedom opens the wide panorama of life and makes one lonely. Hence we are afraid of ourselves like pale ghost shying away from open confrontation of experience. When soul is beset with fear, possibility of freedom becomes sparse and despair enters our soul. Bhatnagar reveals this fact in *Insomnia* :

> What light can reveal
> And dark hide
> When with fear
> The soul is parched
> The marauders have left
> Leaving our freedom
> a scarecrow parked (FF, 20)

Bhatnagar dwells upon the scope of human nature in the figure of Ulysses. He puts up the classical hero before us in a new light. He is a ceaseless wanderer who takes life to be a road. In *Ulysses*, he makes this point clear :

All roads have dead ends
But living soul
Walks out of the body
As white as crane
Laying off he arresting water. (OV, 11)

As a concerned observer Bhatnagar not merely deals with the individual destiny of man but also brings into purview all spheres of life — social, political and philosophical. Everywhere he probes the basic enigma gnawing at human existence. Existentialists have been not to provide pure disinterested statement of truth, but also to free the people of their illusions. Warnock repeatedly points out this faculty of arousing awareness as the basic tent of existentialism. Protest for existentialists, is the means of arousing awareness of the self. According to Blackham, the philosophy of existentialism is not a romantic passion or work of reactionary defence but it excels in protest challenge, warning, and is not an adequate constructive effort. Bhatnagar widens its scope and looks upon protest as liberator : "freeing the creative and constructive in man. This may involve putting fights against the socio-political system of today."[7] Considering that man is the focus of this struggle, Bhatnagar thinks that dignity of man has largely dwindled in the prevailing situations in India. His conception of man has not been derived from any philosophy, theology or literary models of the East or the West but as a vibrant living being responsive to the multidimensional situations around him. Bhatnagar's deep concern for the present loss of human values is a dominant theme in a number of poems from the *Thought Poems* to *The Audible Landscape* and even some of his new poems. In *Nailing by the Wall*, the poet depicts the loss of hope in the present degenerate society :

The lost years of hoped for happiness
Are winter-logged
And the glories of our ancients
A lived out past

The horizons of the present haunt with
desolation
And reek of cancerous corruptions in the bones. (TP, 4)

In the *Way to See a Thing* which Srinivasan calls a characteristic poetic achievement. The poet evokes with vividness many-sided life of an Indian town. Even the description of the seasons unveils the dryness and monotony of modern man which echoes T.S. Eliot's early poetry :

Winter comes in spasm
The hot sun sucks trees of their shadow
Summer winds drown all day dreams
Driving dead dry leaves to the dusty doors
It gets muddy for sneezes
Turning the whole town into a mudatario
Missed by Dante and his purgatario (AR, 28)

Although Bhatnagar finds the general plight of common man gravely deplorable, he is not without hope. His poetry gains strength from his faith that what has been lost can be adequately compensated by greater involvement with emerging new consciousness and conscience. This idea is depicted in the following lines from *History is Sorry Go Round* :

Like phoenix risen from the ashes
The crucified have but kept
The candle of conscience alight
In the deserted temples of forgotten ideals
Can now rise, cleanse and enlighten
The strained glory of man. (AR, 41)

Bhatnagar is fully aware of the state of mind which produced existential anxiety in the modern way of living. He observes :

> A sense of futility and helplessness and degeneracy forms part of the content of modern man's existence caught in network of deception and hypocrisy to go ahead in life; reason has been rendered useless and imagination powerless. Man, therefore, has been rendered merely to go through the motion of living without being alive. The only feeling that one undergoes is of boredom.[8]

On the Cross Road is a memorable poem which exhorts the oppressed masses to come out of the mud and mire of their miserable existence :

> Uproot the sing posts
> That have aged telling faded routes
> And bring down the Milky Way
> For the innocents to tread down. (OV, 18)

Paying rich tributes to Bhatnagar for his poetry enriched with modern perspectives which render it singularly distinct from that of his contemporaries, Srinivasan observes :

> That is partly because of the refreshingly modern perspective that he brings to his perception of man and his circumambient world. Bhatnagar is essentially a radical realist and the directions, he has established, are likely to influence the poetry of eighties.[9]

Although Bhatnagar is actually conscious of the negative principles in the world, yet he is not a negative thinker. He views suffering as an inseparable part of life but does not allow it to overpower him. He says : "Although suffering is a living fact of human predicament one must die of and for it.... If joy cannot stay long why should suffering stay longer."[10]

Martin Heiddegger view death as not total annihilator but as a clue to authentic living. Jaspers and Marcel point toward the ambiguity of the world which invites despair and instigate faith as well. According to Nietzsche and Sartre philosophic and religious faiths are non-existent. Man is both a thing and not a thing. Bhatnagar also realizes the ambiguous nature of experience. We have broken the fetters of slavery but walls of prison house remain. As a result our existence is full of chaos and disturbances.

Like the existentialists Bhatnagar also sees triumph in the great strategy of retreat in nature. Self-retreat is the way to defeat death or enemies. Through the images of Sati and Sanyasi Bhatnagar presents this defiance in his poem *Trees in Autumn* :

> Trees in Autumn go bereft of leaves
> As if by a grand strategy of retreat

To defeat the Neloleonic designs of snow
They lure the marauder away to
Jeering desolation. (AR, 22)

There are a number of poems in which the poet voices his contempt for the violation of human rights. The despicable plight of the children is portrayed in *I Can Question Only My Dreams*. Loss of morality and the havocs of selfish ends are effectively brought out in the poems *New Morality* and *Living Scene*.

Thus entire range of Bhatnagar's poetry there is always the intensest concern for the common man. He raises his voice of revolt against everything that belittles human dignity. Through his poetry his voice rises like volcano to crush, burn and destroy everything that creates obstacles to human progress and glory. I sincerely hope Bhatnagar will sooner or later achieve that goal he has set in his poetry.

REFERENCES

1. J.A. Cuddon (ed.), *Dictionary of Literary Terms* (London : Andre deutsch Ltd., 1977), p. 246.
2. *Ibid.*, p. 247.
3. *Ibid.*
4. Quoted by Mrs P. Kasture in her Article *O.P. Bhatnagar the Poet of Integral Existence, Poetry*, 12 (Berhampur : 1986), pp. 21-22.
5. O.P. Bhatnagar, "Poetry is Tenderness," *Hitvada*, Sunday Magazine, Nagpur : Sept. 26, 1982, p. 1.
6. John D. Wild, *Existentialism as Philosophy* in Sartre's : *A Collection of Critical Essays* (N.J. Prentice Hall, 1962), p. 147.
7. O.P. Bhatnagar, *The Nature and Role of Poetry and Poets in Present Times*. Text of the keynote address delivered at the Asian Poets' Conference (Tokyo, Japan : Nov. 2, 1984), p. 5.
8. *Journal of Literature and Aesthetics*, Vol. II, No. 223, April/July, 1982, p. 80.
9. S. Srinivas, "The Image of Man in the Poetry of O.P. Bhatnagar," *The Vision and the Voice*, Vol. II, p. 168.
10. O.P. Bhatnagar, *Poetry is Tenderness*, *op. cit.*, p. 1.

14

Womanhood Enmeshed in the Web of Tradition and Modernity : A Comparison between Balamani Amma's and Kamala Das's Ideas

—P.S. Radha

The comparative study of Balamani Amma [b. 1909], a renowned poetess in Malayalam and her daughter, Kamala Das [b. 1934], based on their ideas of womanhood reveals that the status of women in India is ever changing and the change is from deification to utter subservience. Balamani Amma's poems highlight the traditional ideas related to womanhood, which are characterized by consideration of righteousness, duty and virtue. Kamala Das's poems, on the other hand, seek to expose how the old social values are repudiated and destroyed by new values of social justice and equality, which pose a challenge to the traditional values. Balamani Amma revitalizes India's past by assigning conventional roles to women in the family, whereas Kamala Das's poems expose the dichotomy between the conceptual and the existential aspects of womanhood in the country.

The study of Balamani Amma's poems reveals that she is rooted in the Indian tradition. She belonged to an aristocratic matrilineal Nair joint-family, which attached much sanctity to human relationships. She grew up with a spirit of acceptance and complacency, without daring to question the traditional standards. These traditional value systems have influenced Balamani

Amma's ideas of womanhood. Men and women in her poems harmoniously respond to the traditional Indian thinking. Motherhood becomes for the poetess a spiritual transformation of wifehood, a unified and undivided experience.

In Kamala Das, the Indian conservative crust cracks, challenging the orthodoxies of tradition and defying the patriarchal social norms. She is concerned with the "here and now" of things and her poems show the poetess's full awareness of the existential reality of woman as 'indriyartha', an instrument of pleasure in the hands of men. While Balamani Amma is concerned with the idealistic, Kamala Das is bothered about the experiential.

In India, the concept of Ardhanariswara conceives of God-heard as half-man and half-woman, representing the integral view of Hinduism about the relation between man and woman. Complying with this Hindu elevation of the feminine principle, in Balamani Amma's poems, man and woman act as complementary to each other and their heterogeneous relationship is one of harmony and peace. As cultural influence is bound to act upon our more intimate as well as our social selves, one finds that women in Balamani Amma's poems are concerned with such core values as love, fidelity and integrity. The deep and manifold rootedness of their life in the tradition of our country imposes upon women greater restrictions and tighter controls.

In the poem 'Deeparadhana'[1] [Adoration with Lamps], Balamani Amma shows the mode and ground on which empirical and transcendental values are related in a Hindu woman's life and how she can effect a positive transition from the one to the other through the familial role of wife. At dusk, as is the custom in Hindu families, the speaker lights a lamp; after some time she closes the door, lest the wind should put the lamp out. She soon enters into a prayerful, meditative trance, in an attempt to have a union with the sublime essence of the universe. But the universe tells her to turn her face and listen :

> Like the heart of the cosmos pulsating,
> I hear, clear and swift, the foot-steps
> Of my beloved, Love incarnate,
> Waiting anxious to get the door open.
>
> [My translation, SP, 40]

Though the speaker is distracted by the voice of the universe, which keeps reminding her that the light which she seeks, resides here and now, and not far away, she refuses to pay heed to it and continues her adoration with lamps and flowers, in her endeavour to participate in the divine grace. Soon a transformation takes place within her :

> While the cosmos peers at me through the vents
> In the thatched roof, I remember
> Those lustrous eyes, languidly longing,
> That wait outside for me
> And the lamp, lit beside me darts
> like snake's red tongue in the gloom cast around.
>
> [My translation, SP, 41]

As the trance-like state which the woman was trying to generate within her appears horrifying, she runs and opens the door and the wind puts out the lamp. But there comes the realization that even if the lamp is extinguished, there is the representative of the Divine, who is to light her life's path. She sees her husband waiting for her in the rose garden. His smile transcends every object; she bows her head and she looks like a new bride. [SP 42]

"Deeparadhana" glorifies marital love and conjugal bliss and explains the kernel of wifely devotion. The wife sees in her husband the image of God. For her, he exists only in relation to God, and it is this belief that sustains their relationship. God manifests Himself to the wife through the husband and his soul to her is an image of the divine goodness and sanctity.

To quote from *Ramayana* in this context, it is worthwhile to remember Anasuya's words to Sita, who resolved to accompany her husband and share life of suffering and distress as that was the proper ideal for an Aryan woman to pursue. Sita appreciated Anasuya's words and replied :

> I know that there is no other austerity or penance ordained for a woman than service to her husband. This is how Savithry, yourself and Rohini have achieved ever-lasting fame.[2]

Balamani Amma often dramatizes the Indian traditional ideas of womanhood through her poems, by emphasizing the importance of chastity and austerity in woman's life as she exists only in relation to her husband. In "Deeparadhana", the woman, by her divine intuition, endows the husband with that divine nature, which she sees in God. It is suggested that she is able to lift herself to a higher plane, far above human limitations, because of her close communion with God and not from the conscious exercise of her will. The change, thus wrought, transforms the wife as well as the husband, that he is no longer an ordinary man, but a being with a divine nature innate in him.

Kamala Das, on the other hand, is aware of the experiential realities which woman faces in the world. Being highly perceptive, gender-injustice has become a disturbing concern for her, as she finds the society biased against woman, who is still enslaved, exploited and sold as a commonly. Hence, in her poems, the traditional concepts of feminine behaviour and socialization vanish and the roles of woman as chaste daughter and dutiful wife collapse. In Kamala Das's poetry, one hears the voice of a wounded woman, who is ill-at-ease with this world, who lays bare the dangers that lurk and await woman in the world of male supremacy.

Prabhakar Machwe, in his *Four Decades of Indian Literature* quoting Carl Sadburg's definition of poetry that it is "the journal of a sea-animal living on land, trying to fly in the air," observes that the poet is "a maladjusted being, eternally protesting against his environment, out of place everywhere, at home nowhere."[3] What Sandburg means is that the poet, living in a tense world of strenuous and difficult metaphysics, finds himself at war with his environment and becomes an isolated voice and, being utterly crippled, has the awareness of his isolation.

Kamala Das's condition is not much different from that of her counterpart described by Sandburg. She is caught up in the confusion of values of her age and as an artist, she attempts to invent a system of attitudes and beliefs for herself, that will give meaning to the ideas of womanhood in her poems. Here, the mind and intellect of Kamala Das are seen not to proceed beyond the routine problems of household and family structure to the metaphoric and symbolic extensions of meanings seen in Balamani Amma's poems. Kamala Das writes in 'Composition'[4]:

> Only those who like to listen,
> listen.
> What I narrate are the ordinary
> events of an
> ordinary life. [OP, 7]

Kamala Das's poems are the frank utterances of many women, whose sounds are muffled voices, because they do not have the capacity or audacity to question or rebel. What they keep hushed either due to fear of shame or to uphold tradition is articulated by Kamala Das most vehemently. As Linda Hess notes :

> Kamala Das's subjects are the things that most people need, desire, constantly think about, and are terribly afraid of. She writes of love, sex, deprivation, fulfilment, separation, and the death process as revealed in the day-to-day deterioration of senses and emotions. To these subjects she brings an honesty that is sometimes brutal and sometimes pathetic, but nearly always moving.[5]

The actual life-experiences of many women who have no other choice except to surrender themselves to male mastery or to sacrifice willingly or unwillingly their legitimate rights, thus become the theme for many of Kamala Das's poems. These poems show an increased awareness of the sterner realities of life, which women face in their marital lives. That means, Kamala Das, refuses to inherit an attitude and a philosophy which condition her mother's poems and which are unquestioned by millions of Indians.

For Kamala Das too, love is the mainstay of woman's life. Like Balamani Amma, she attaches much importance to love, but very often it is denied to her in her personal as well as social life. Hence, her poems become a search for love in its purest form, love of a higher kind, which involves the soul, and perhaps is never realized in this life. Her maiden volume

Summer in Calcutta[6] speaks of her quest for true love. Eunice de Souza comments, "She writes about love, or rather, the failure of love or the absence of love with the obsessiveness of a woman who can realize her being fully only through love."[7] According to Kamala Das, a woman's quest for a love-life is rooted in emotional recognition, acceptance and appreciation. In "An Apology to Gautama' [SC, 19] she states it vividly :

> ...but in your arms I must today
> Lie, and find an oasis where memories'
> Sad winds do not so much blow, and I must
> Hear you say, I love, I love, I love.... [SC, 19]

It is an enchanting experience for woman to be cuddled by a man in whose hands she feels accepted as a *person*, and not treated as a *thing*, to be discarded after use. In "The Suicide"[8] the woman voices her desire :

> I want to be simple
> I want to be loved
> And
> If love is not to be had
> I want to be dead.... [TD, 2]

This shows that, according to Kamala Das, love is a wonderful stimulus for woman and woman's love is more intense than man's. For her, it is a "cloyless thing",[9] a genuine emotion, far removed from sensuality or lust. Hence, as Anisur Rahman points out, her feminine sensibility is :

> not to be explored in her frank confessions of her sexual life or in detailed descriptions of female organs. It is expressly manifested in her attitude to love in the ecstasy she experiences in receiving love and the agony which he feels when jilted in it.[10]

The poem "Love" [SC, 30] is a fine exposition of the emotional aspect of a woman's love-life, which provides the basis for building a healthy man-woman relationship :

> Until I found you,
> I wrote verse, drew pictures,
> And, went out with friends
> For walks....

Now that I love you
Curied like an old mongrel
My life lies, content,
In you.... [SC, 30]

The poetess does realize that love is the greatest treasure in a woman's life, and the one and the only weak spot in her is an entanglement in the affair of the heart. Love makes her life take a different turn. While languishing in man's protection, she explores new frontiers of inter-personal relationships. As Bijay Kumar Das says, "She [Kamala Das] is in the main a poet of love, of love from the woman's point of view, to whom the centre is not the blind worship of the husband but the consummation of love."[11] Through "Love" Kamala Das asserts that woman's need for masculine care and protection is inborn in her and her life finds its fulfilment. In delicateness and submissiveness she experiences while under masculine command. Thus, it is clear that Kamala Das, like her mother, regards true man-woman relationship as a life-filling experience for woman.

In Balamani Amma's poems like "Prabhathathil" [In the Dawn, SP, 43-45] and "Adukkalayil" [In the Kitchen, SP, 46-49] the emotion of "love" is tied to the country's culture in such strong ways that love becomes an enrichment for the partners, each enlarging oneself through the other. In "Prabhathathil" the speaker is preparing herself to slip into a spiritual mood in order to glorify the greatness of the universe. The venue chosen for this meditative exercise is the bank of the river. But she notices :

As the ascendant sun brightens up the sky
In come the thoughts of dear and near
The memories of family life surge in the heart
Crescendoing to a philosophic climax.
[My translation, SP, 44]

Entering a unique, auspicious disposition, the woman tries to partake in the Godly grace that pervades the universe. But soon, she finds herself enmeshed in thoughts of her sweet home :

While the river waves sparkle and shimmer
In the golden rays of the Sun, there shines

In my bosom too, the silhoutte of my home,
Bathed in the same glory. I hear the anklets
Tinkle, of my children, the shoots of my life,
Who run here and there playing; and I see
My beloved, waiting for me in the street
with a flower, newly sprung!

[My translation, SP, 45]

The above lines exemplify the fact that, according to Balamani Amma, household work itself is a kind of adoration for woman and any supplication based on love, sacrifice and selflessness is the secret of a successful married life. She is enlightened with the wisdom, "I realize, any thought about home/Is, for housewife, a prayer raised to God." [My translation, SP, 45]. No doubt, for Balamani Amma, the household work is an immediate and concrete experience; yet, through that she aims at a life of salvation, which is transcendent, because she is sure that she can transmute her family life into a divine, mystical experience. Here again, what Balamani Amma expounds is the duty ethics of the *Bhagavadgita* :

> Do then thy allotted work, for action is better than inaction; even the maintenance of thy physical life cannot be effected without action.
>
> Save work done as and for a sacrifice this world is in bondage to work. Therefore, O son of Kunti [Arjuna], do thy work as a sacrifice, becoming free from all attachment.[12]

As the *Bhagavadgita* exhorts that all work is to be done in a spirit of sacrifice for the sake of the Divine, so too Balamani Amma believes that salvation cannot be attained through inaction or meditation. According to her, the temporal, common place experiences must gain a universality through woman's selfless sacrifice, which in turn, must illumine her soul and invest her life with a special meaning and purpose.

In both "Adukkalayil" and "Prabhathathil" the wife, instead of being locked in the cell of the ego, is able to participate in the life and existence of her husband, who, for her, becomes an extra window to the outside world, because of her altruistic love for him. In both these poems, the poet captures the subtle moods and graces of love in man-woman relationship. It is not physical or sexual love that is glorified, but love of a celestial kind, where, through the husband, the wife seeks salvation. There is no rupture or nonfulfilment in the relationship, but perfect amity and tranquility. Though Balamani Amma's women are submissive and vulnerable models of perfect obedience, in them are bred the finer elements of Indian family life. They believe that a life of selflessness and self-sacrifice is superior to one of selfishness and self-indulgence. They do not question or theories about these moral excellences, but the core of Indian moral concepts is intuitively assimilated into their behavioural patterns of daily life.

For Kamala Das, her early marriage at the age of fifteen, which shattered all her juvenile dreams, came as the greatest tragedy of her life. She confesses, "A broken marriage was as distasteful, as horrifying as an attack of leprosy."[13] Her writings, apart from being personal confessions, are the tangible outpourings of all women in a male-dominated society who experience the denial of personhood. The plurality of selves revealed through Kamala Das's poems makes her cry out in "Loud Posters" [SC, 23] that "I am today a creature turned inside/out" and as a poet, she locates the areas of struggle and exposes the damage done to the female psyche. So intense is her participation in the day-to-day realities that she breaks all codes of decorum and morality in her writings. To quote from "Loud Posters" again :

> ...I've stretched my two dimensional
> Nudity on sheets on weeklies, monthlies,
> Quarterlies, a sad sacrifice. I've put
> My private voice away, adopted the
> Typewriter's click as my only speech. I
> Click-click, click-click tiresomely into your
> Ears, stranger, though you may have no need of
> Me, I go on and on, not knowing why....
>
> [SC, 23]

Kamala Das analyses love in the modern social context and argues that it is the pivot of woman's oppression today. She is vehement and vociferous in her protest against male supremacy, social discrimination and marginalization of women. In "Of Calcutta" Kamala Das writes :

> I was sent away, to protect a family's
> Honour to save a few cowards, to defend some
> Abstractions, sent to another city to be
> A relative's wife, a hausfrau for his home, and
> A mother for his sons, yet another nodding
> Doll for his parlour, a walkie-talkie one to
> Warm his bed at night....[14]

These lines reveal Kamala Das's revolt against brutalization and oppression that become women's lot with their marriage. According to Niranjan Mohanty, "Of Calcutta" exposes "the intricacies of inner pangs stemming from marriage" :

> She is iconoclastic in her approach to marriage. She treats 'marriage' as 'a game of cruelty.' Her female ego comes to the surface when she ruefully depicts the loss of liberty.[15]

Like many women, "In silence I lay at night and/Thought of human love," only to come to the conclusion that :

> Here in my husband's home,
> I am a trained circus dog
> Jumping my routine hoops each day, where is my soul,
> My spirit, where the muted tongues of my desire ?
> [CP, 59]

The above lines mirror Kamala Das's open resentment of and revolt against the traditional tutelage given to women in marriage. Bereft of freedom, the wife becomes a trained circus dog, jumping to the tunes of the master-husband. If Balamani Amma glorifies the blissful experience of love, Kamala Das speaks of love resulting in the destruction of individual, or at least in an emotional cynicism that makes it difficult, if not impossible, for woman to love again.

In Balamani Amma's poems, there is no rejection of male dominance because she does not feel dominated. Hence, there is no startling frankness in her utterances. She never regards the traditional roles of woman as wife and mother as fetters that keep her chained. If Balamani Amma spiritualizes her domestic experiences and glorifies the bliss of conjugal love, Kamala Das, as seen in "Of Calcutta" speaks of love, resulting in emotional barrenness and destruction of woman's self-worth. To quote S.C. Harrex, "Many of Kamala Das's poems epitomize the dilemma of the modern Indian woman who attempts to free herself, sexually and domestically, from the role bondage sanctioned by the past."[16]

"The Old Playhouse" [OP, 1-2], "Loud Posters" [SC, 23], "Gino" [OP, 13-14], "Glass" [OP, 21-22], "The Looking Glass" [TD, 25] are all poems, where love seen in the modern social context becomes the real cause of woman's oppression. The culture and the atmosphere in these poems are saturated with sexual polarity, so much so that in the interest of the male society, the female's "emotional" aspect is forgotten.[17] In the "The Old Playhouse" the formula-based working pattern of the wife is pictured thus :

> I was taught to break saccharine into your tea and To offer at the right moment the vitamins. Cowering Beneath your monstrous ego, I ate the magic loaf and Became a dwarf.
>
> [OP, 1]

The conventional role which the wife is expected to play is caricatured here by Kamala Das and it incapacitates the female, eventually making her a puppet, dancing to the music of the male's "monstrous ego." S.C. Harrex comments thus on the above lines, "Any woman who has suffered at the hands of a selfish domineering male is likely to derive bitter satisfaction from the irony and pain of such lines." [KDSW, 170]

Balamani Amma, on the contrary, eulogises the household duties as an offering at the feet of the husband-lord. Her poems such as "Ambalathilekku" [To the Temple, SP, 64-66], "Ammayum Makanum" [Mother and Son, SP, 8-10], "Kavyamrutham" [The Nectar of Poetry, SP, 6-7], and "Mathruchumbanam" [Mother's Kiss, SP, 3-5] are gleaming examples, where woman as wife and mother, aims at *moksha*, the religious goal of salvation, which can be identified with the virtues of a saint.

In Balamani Amma's poems, woman is bewitched by a religious bent of mind and finds joy and contentment in her roles as wife and mother. "Vadhuvinodu" [To the Bride, SP, 70-71] embodies the poet's advice to the brides who are about to enter into wedlock. The emotional closeness between the protective mother and the anxious daughter makes the mother the daughter's confidant and counsellor. Before the newly wed daughter departs to her husband's home, the mother advises :

> That flower of love, oozing honey,
> A blossom made for adoration of the Lord,
> That venue of marriage, a place for a rite,
> An altar made for sacrifice of the Ego
> That conjugal bliss, leading to self-esteem
> A ladder reaching out to self-realization
> Let that strength of the spirit of Indian woman
> Be embedded in you.
>
> [My translation, SP, 71]

The most practical preparation for a happy marital life, according to Balamani Amma, is a religious discipline, whereby reason enlightens the lady regarding the role she is to play with her husband, while exploring the meaning of life together. Her selfless devotion helps her in the attainment of the spiritual essence of life, through the person of her husband, who becomes for her a personal divinity. Balamani Amma elevates woman in her poems to the position of *sanyasinis* because the central motif in her poem is wife's undivided allegiance and loyalty towards her husband, which can be regarded as a *bhakta's* devotion to her Lord.

For Kamala Das, the marital bond designates a relationship based on falsity, pretensions and insincerity. She suggests that the traditional society of Balamani Amma is falling off around her, giving way to a new loose set up, where relationships are ambiguous and not permanent or life-long. "Apology to Goutama" [SC, 19], "The Freaks" [SC, 10], "A Relationship" [SC, 18], "The Prisoner", [SC, 18], "The Stone Age" [OP, 51], "Forest Fire" [OP, 39] are all instances in point, where the poetess speaks of unconsummated love. In "Apology to Goutama' the wife tells the husband that it was another man who made her lonely :

...and yet Goutama
That other owns me; while your arms hold,
My woman-form, his hurting arms
Hold my very soul. [SC, 19]

The idea of marriage as the ethical law of God, which finds its traditional expression in the poems of Balamani Amma, is detraditionalized in the above lines. Here marriage is not based on love or mutual fidelity and as the partners do not recognise the divine order of marriage, the relationship is not binding. For Balamani Amma, marriage bond is sacrosanct and indissoluble, whereas for Kamala Das clandestine sex is pictured as yielding greater and richer pleasure than socially permitted marital sex. For Balamani Amma, sexual relationship between husband and wife is not simply sexual intercourse, but an act which involves the union of two minds and emotions as well as bodies, which thus becomes a total, complete union.

According to the Hindu Dharmasastras, the wife is *ardhangini* [half of man] and the bushand is *bhartri* [householder] because he is to support his wife. She is the husband's best of friends and also the source of *dharma* [righteousness], *artha* [wealth] and *kama* [love], leading him ultimately to *moksha* [salvation]. Marriage for the traditional Hindu is one of the essential *samskaras* [sacrament] which exalts the wife from the position of a *grihapatni* [housewife] to *dharmapatni* [righteous wife]. Balamani Amma addresses the parents on the day their first child is born in the poem 'Benediction'[18] thus :

Oh parents ! today is your marriage complete.
There tender hands can alone
Make strong your marriage ties.
These ruddy lips can alone
Brighten the kumkum mark on mother's brow.
[TP, 2]

The relationship between husband and wife is religious and holy in character and their union is an eternal one, lifting the wife to the pedestal of a *yogini.* The mother has nurtured a new human being, who is the evidence of the love she and her husband share. The child is an extension of the parents, the touchstone of their pure love and the poetess believes, the child alone can weld them together forever. In contrast to Kamala Das's poems, here the intimacy is formed and maintained on the basis of reciprocity and fidelity, resulting in a lasting life of togetherness.

Kamala Das's counsel to husbands and wives is arresting :

> Husbands and wives,
> here is any advice to you.
> Obey each other's crazy commands,
> ignore the sane.
> Turn your home into a merry
> dog-house,
> marriage is meant to be all this
> anyway,
> being arranged in
> most humorous heaven. [OP, 8]

Kamala Das knows well that reality corresponds to the idealized concept of marriage as pictured by Balamani Amma. She does not attack the institution of marriage, says Anne Brewsler :

> ...perhaps because of her strong link with traditional forms, she is well aware of the emotional ossification that it can produce. She appears to find a solution in personal effort rather than a restructuring of the society.[19]

If Kamala Das questions and seems to distort the traditional concept of marriage, which is glorified by Balamani Amma, it is because of her awareness of the difference between assumptions and actuals. She is not a radical feminist who repudiates man, but she advocates a union rooted in fidelity, understanding and love. What she means is that male body has become a trap for woman, in the poem "I Shall Some Day" [SC, 52], she calls male body, her "betrayer's arms," or the "nest of familiar scorn." She writes in "The Morning at Apollo Pier" thus :

> They tell me that your love is
> A morass where I must sink, if not

today,
Tomorrow.[20]

As Prabhat Kumar Pandeya writes in the essay, "The Pink Pulsating Words : The Woman's Voice in Kamala Das's Poetry" :

> [Kamala Das] is not a woman libber, for after all questionings and probing, she realizes that man's love is the last resort even though it may be crushing her own being and personality. It seems that after all freedom and wandering woman has to come back to man's love and even his scorn.[21]

It is perhaps the hopeless struggle for an active, emancipated femininity and the underlying hostility towards selfish men in general that make Kamala Das picture the husband-figure in her poems as an ugly one, stimulating nausea and repulsion.

In Balamani Amma's poems, the husband-figure is defied. His presence is felt rather than seen. He is at the core of all her poems dealing with family relationships, rather omnipresent, unseen, yet exercising a very powerful influence on all the members of the household. For Balamani Amma, wife is *jivatma*, the empirical self and husband is *paramatma*, the transcendental self. The union between the two sublimates the former leading to "Brahma-realization" or "God-realization."

To conclude, this paper is an attempt to bring out the two diverging trends in Malayalam poetry and Indian-English poetry through the study of the poems of a mother and her daughter. It demonstrates that traditional ideas of womanhood and contemporary realities of life and thinking set up areas of tension in thinking and feeling. The lofty ideas of womanhood, glorified and sung about in tradition, and the real demands of modern life on women as well as the reactions of women to modern situations have generated a confusing and bewildering spectrum of womanhood; one cannot easily ignore the traditional values, but one cannot, at the same time, live up to them in real life. Thus, if womanhood becomes resplendent in Balamani Amma's poems, in Kamala Das's poems it is problematized, being caught in the medley of modernity.

NOTES AND REFERENCES

1. Balamani Amma, *Sopanam* [Kozhikode : Mathrubhumi Printing and Publishing Company, 1966], 39-42. In subsequent references abbreviated to SP.
2. N. Chandrasekhara Aiyer, *Valmiki Ramayana* [Bombay : Bharatiya Vidya Bhavan, 1988] 58.
3. Prabhakar Machwe, *Four Decades of Indian Literature* [New Delhi : Chetana Publications, 1976] 55.
4. Kamala Das, *The Old Playhouse* [Madras : Orient Longman, 1973]. Hereafter cited as OP.
5. Linda Hess, "Post-independence Indian Poetry in English," *Quest*, No. 49, Spring 1966, 37.
6. Kamala Das, *Summer in Calcutta* [New Delhi : Everest Press, 1965]. Later cited as SC.
7. Eunice de Souza, "Kamala Das, Gauri Deshpande, Mamta Kalia", *Contemporary Indian Poetry in English : An Assessment and Selection*, cd. Saleem Peeradina [Bombay : Macmillan, 1972] 85.
8. Kamala Das, *The Descendants* [Calcutta : Writers' Workshop, 1967]. Later abbreviated to TD.
9. William T. Robinson, *Woman : Her Sex and Love Life* [New York : Eugenies Publishing Company, 1931] 324.
10. Anisur Rahman, *Expressive Form in the Poetry of Kamala Das* [New Delhi : Abhinav Publications, 1981] 4.
11. Bijay Kumar Das, *Modern Indo-English Poetry* [Bareilly : Prakash Book Depot, 1982] 44.
12. S. Radhakrishnan, trans., *The Bhagavadgita* [Bombay : Blakie and Son Publishers, 1982] 135.
13. Kamala Das, *My Story* [New Delhi : Sterling Publishers, 1988]. Later cited as MS.
14. Kamala Das, *Collected Poems* [Trivandrum : Navakerala Printers, 1984] 58-59. Later abbreviated to C.P.
15. Niranjan Mohanty, "The Feminist Perspective : Poetry of Kamala Das," *Malayalam Literary Survey,* Vol. 16, No. 2, Apr.-Jan. 1993, 49.
16. S.C. Harrex, "The Strange Case of Matthew Arnold in a Sari : An Introduction to Kamala Das," *Kamala Das : A Selection with Essays on her Work,* ed. S.C. Harrex and Vincent O'Sullivan [Adelaide : CRNLE, 1986] 163. Later citer as KDSW.
17. Shulamith Fire Stone, *The Dialectic of Sex* [London : Jonathan Cape Limited, 1971] 42.
18. Balamani Amma, *Thirty Poems* [Madras : Orient Longman, 1970] 2. Later cited as TP.

19. Anne Brewster, "'The Freedom to Decompose' : The Poetry of Kamala Das," *The Journal of Indian Writing in English,* Vol. 18, No. 1 and 2, Jan.-July 1980, 99.
20. Gaurri Deshpande, ed., *An Anthology of Indian English Poetry* [New Delhi : Hind Pocket Books, n.d.] 35.
21. Prabhat Kumar Pandeya, "The Pink Pulsating Words : The Woman's Voice in Kamala Das's Poetry," *Indian Literature Today*, Vol. 2, *Poetry and Fiction,* ed., R.K. Dhavan [New Delhi : Prestige Books, 1994] 74.

15

Quest for Self-Realisation in Nissim Ezekiel's Poetry

—M.K. Pandey

It is generally believed that Indian poetry in English, having passed the phase of imitation and national self-consciousness has attained maturity through independence and individuality. This self-consciousness and awareness has played an important role in the writing of modern Indian poetry in English. Nissim Ezekiel, a widely known contemporary poet of India has strived hard to adhere to the principle of self-awareness in his famous book *Collected Poems* 1952-88. Commenting about the quest for self in Ezekiel's poetry, Gieve Patel observes in the Introduction :

> When he writes his poetry he teaches,
> this time largely himself. In all these
> contexts the pedagogic tone is relieved,
> even subverted by self-directed irony,
> subdued passion, and simple, direct concern
> for what's at hand.[1]

In spite of this, one has reasons to believe that Ezekiel's quest for self-realisation has become the underlying theme of his poetry and can be perceived in the several poems included in the significant volume *Collected Poems* 1952-1988. Though poems specially included in his *Collected Poems*, first *A Time to Change* (1952) has a clear concern with spirituality and self-realisation and *Hymns in Darkness* (1976) and *Latter Day-Psalms* (1982) are also the best example of this theme. The marvellous poems such as "The Egoist's Prayers", or "Hymns in Darkness" from *Hymns in Darkness* are ironic exposes of the self-deceptions of modern day seeker and their concern is not directly with the mystical experience. The poem "Latter Day Psalms" based on the poet's readings from the psalms, is also concerned partly with the poet's experience of self-realisation.

However, Ezekiel's first volume of verse included in *Collected Poems* 1952-88, *A Time to Change* most directly addresses the poet's quest for self-realisation but it is uncertain whether the poet ultimately attains his goal or not. Unlike the other mystics who are fully realised, one's impression of Ezekiel is of a serious, though wavering commitment, which is yet not fully realised. But his quest for self-realisation is seen most obviously in the poem "Something to Pursue." What he seeks is nothing but high endeavour :

> "with intensities
> of feeling and of thought,
> That I may see myself
> No longer unresolved
> But definite as morning,
> Moving to fruition
> When the season comes."[2]

He is a 'man aspiring to the Good, which may be God', and the answer to his quest lies somewhere in the unique poem "Prayer and Poetry, Poetry and Prayer." Here the poet is trying to attain a way of life through poetry emerging from the heart and something more beyond this :

> "A man may follow it
> Through works or poetry,
> From works to poetry
> Or from poetry to something else." (*C.P.*, p. 14)

The poet pursues passionately nothing but 'this lucid utterance, of unambiguous speech' and the 'limpid style of life, whose texture is poetry. Ezekiel like Dom Moraes is not accepting God as it is but contemplating about Him, and as he points out in "A Time to Change" the title poem that "practising a singing and a talking voice. Is all the creed a man of God requires" or as he aspires in the middle of the poem :

> The pure invention or the perfect poem,
> Precise communication of a thought,
> Love reciprocated to a quiver,
> Flawless doctrines, certainty of God.
>
> (*C.P.*, p. 5)

Most of the critics have pointed out that there is an underlying spiritual quest in his poetry. But being a Indian poet, Ezekiel's own judgement about his poetry has become the chief characteristic of his personality where one can get a glimpse of poet's own self-conviction. As the poet himself describes :

> "I am not a religious or even a moral person in any conventional sense. Yet, I've always felt myself to be religious and moral in some sense. The gap between these two statements is the essential sphere of my poetry.[3]

However in *A Time to Change* poem after poem, Ezekiel is trying his best to obliterate the obstacles coming all along in the fulfilment of his dreams. The poet's own self-diagnosis can be seen when he describes that he is "corrupted by the things imagined" ("A Time to Change") but in the important poem "The Double Horror" :

> "I am corrupted by the world, continually
> Reduced to something less than human by the crowd.

Ezekiel's striving to become a finished man compels him to the self-analysis and introspection we come across in some of his poems. For instance in the poem "The Warm", seeing a warm crawling blindly to a drier spot after the rain, he speculates :

> "Oh God! To think that I
> By such absurd and devious routes should reach
> My destination. I there anywhere
> A warm blinder than I have been." (*C.P.*, p. 10)

But in "Words in a Gentle Wind", he comes to know "The empty zone within" and in "Commitment", "I am reduced/To appetites and godlessness." Keeping in view this characteristic of Ezekiel, Makarand R. Paranjape beautifully remarks that "such relentless self-scrutiny and castigation continues unabated through the other collection as well. Hence, the obstacles in the way of the poet's self-realisation, in his own eyes seem formidable."[4]

Expanding his poetic sensibility, Ezekiel at the end of his volume, *A Time to Change* comes to final resolution. The last two poems "Declaration" and "Encounter" suggest a transformation similar to the mystical experience in which the poet ultimately understands the meaning of life. For instance :

> And took, the liberation! The poise of
> being one with God, the precious quietude
> of blood, the aftermath of bold acceptance!
>
> Intimation of some final good comes in
> surrender; waiting instead of seeking,
> Wanting nothing, being nothing, like a
> Crab or Kingfisher by the water, in the
> Sun, and lighted up within.
>
> (*C.P.*, p. 34)

Here it seems that the poet does not surrender completely, attaining the "poise of being one with God" and the impact of this clear realisation can be seen in the rest of his poetry. In the last poem of this volume "Encounter" too some illuminating experiences are vigorously suggested : The poet realises that the question itself suggests the answer, that it is not always necessary to ask questions. An old pattern of the mind is broken. A mystery is divulged in the answer of the unknown converser, simply life, merge with its rhythm. The key seems to be in ever-moving, flowing with life, taking refuse only in "living images", not clinging to dead or fassilized ideas of yesterday. Wordsworth finally comprehends that the sole aim of life is to live harmoniously with the universe and to being one with its eternal laws.

Moreover, in *A Time to Change* Ezekiel is concerned with morality in life, and other burning issues of the day haunt him without end. The journey of the 'Self' becomes a metaphor in his poetry. This metaphor is further carried to its logical conclusion in his subsequent book of verse, *The Third* and *Hymns in Darkness*. Ezekiel has learnt from W.B. Yeats how to compose poems about the self while keeping away from it. In *The Third*, he takes the stance of a detached observer and discusses personal emotions and conduct intellectually in obstractions. For instance the poem "Portrait" in *The Third* presents the predicament of the modern man including the poet himself.

"Beneath his daily strategy,
Reflected in his suffering face
I see his dim identity,
A small, deserted, holy place. (*C.P.*, p. 87)

Ezekiel's quest for realisation seems to be diffident but recollecting his own poetic talent he becomes successful in discovering the truth whether about himself or about others which is his objective. He really believes that :

"Myself examined frightens me...
I have long watched myself
.. ..
I have heard the endless silent dialogue
Between the self-protective self
And the self naked."
("What Frightens Me," *C.P.*, p. 106)

But in his second phase of self-realisation Ezekiel's doubt and ambivalence of early poetry constitute elements of his later knowledge because his poetry, through variations, repetitions and the increasingly open-ended nature of his vision, becomes a record of the growth of a mind acquiring a more complex and inclusive knowledge. His most recent work *Hymns in Darkness* is a poetry of process and growth blending reason and intuition. Most of the poems of this volume are simple, direct intensely evocative and self-satisfying. The poet does not tell us about the nature of readers he writes for. But he is certainly 'a man speaking to men'. His railway clerk opens his heart to the reader and speaks in the tone of great intimacy; for instance :

"I am never neglecting my responsibility,
I am discharging it properly,
I am doing my duty,

> but who is appreciating?
> Nobody, I am telling you. (*C.P.*, p. 184)

Ezekiel is a philosophical poet and proceeds systematically in the treatment of his subject. Like Chaucer, in the famous poem "Guru", for instance, he tells about a saint, sketches the inward story of the man, and finally strikes a deep note. How philosophically, the poet broods over the lot of modern human beings :

> If saints are like this
> What hope is there then for us? (*C.P.*, p. 192)

Ezekiel is a great love-poet and in his poetry he has dealt with his own awareness about the love relationship. The marvellous lyric "poem of the Separation" included in *Hymns in Darkness* shows greater detachment and maturity than the lyrics of the earlier volume. While comparing the reaction in the lover's life with the blast of a bomb, the poet becomes introspective and remembers his beloved who has broken with him :

> To judge by memory alone
> Our love was happy
> When the bombs burst in Kashmir;
> My life had burst
> and merged in yours. (*C.P.*, p. 195)

Ezekiel's poetic talent is perhaps at its best; his tour be force being the disanuing irony. The way information about pictures in a book reaches the poet is meaningful. It is an amusing situation when poet speaks in the beginning of the poem :

> "My daughter tells my wife
> Who tells my mother
> Who tells me." (*C.P.*, p. 200)

Ezekiel's appeal is for a growing knowledge which can make of his place an 'environment'. The environment in which he lives, has a genuine meaning for him. India becomes somewhere to reduce to survive, where he is not imprisoned by time, place or idea. The poet in the verse "The Egoist's Progus" advocates that India is indispensable for him :

"Confiscate my passport, lord,
I don't want to go abroad
Let me find my say
Where I belong." (*C.P.*, p. 213)

However, Ezekiel's poetry revels his primary concern with understanding of the meaning of his life and attaining self-realisation. Poetry seems to be the means to this goal. In the process of pursuing his quest, he is acutely conscious of his own failings and self-deceptions, yet he finds himself preserved frequently. No other poet than Ezekiel has felt ultimately the secret truth of restoration of the soul while confessing about the path of self-righteousness in the latest poem "Latter Day Psalms" where poet seems to be contented by his achievement and scrutiny of the sole self-realisation.

REFERENCES

1. *Collected Poems* 1952-1988, Nissim Ezekiel. New Delhi : O.U.P. 1989; rpt. 1992, p. xvii.
2. *Ibid.*, p. 14. Citations in the body of the text refer to this edition.
3. Quoted in Inder Nath Kher's "Introduction to Nissim Ezekiel," Issue, *Journal of South Asian Literature*, 11 (Spring Summer 1976), p. 5.
4. *Mysticism in Indian English Poetry* (New Delhi : B.R. Publishing Corporation, 1988), p. 200.

16

The Poetry of Maha Nand Sharma

—*V.K. Arora*

In the history of human civilization, there has been a multitude of conscious intellectuality, devotion to the Almighty. The meaningful process of obedience created epics and myths, oracles and legends. The power and the glory, the mysteries and the miracles helped to visualize manifold images through graceful poetry, an unquestionable relation between man and God. It has become almost essential to review easier communication with myths to embrace a new pattern in the journey of life. One, who dedicates spiritual insight to the grandeur of the mightiest, is sure to find place in the field of sublime literature. Maha Nand Sharma is one of the poets among a few in contemporary India to achieve a rare distinction. A Rudraksha Rosary (1987) is a grand presentation of Lord Shiva as one virtuous vagabond sitting high above the mythical time and space. It ratiocinates sublime manifestation of oriental legends of the Hindus mysteriously held around the very image beyond the measure of rituals and supernaturals. "Invocation" (pp. 3-4) is a departure to reach common readers assuming a colour of reality. The rosary around the neck of Lord Shiva symbolizes His mighty powers to punish evils :

> "My laws know no excuse," replied Shiva,
> "Between the high and low they raise no walls.
> A monstrous lie you told, you must be punished."
>
> (Book-I, Lines 287-289)

There is virtue in truthfulness and in the first book on Trinity. The poet recalls the story of mankind. The sad tale of Sati (in

Book-II) incorporates insult to the womenfolk, a never ending process of shame on human society, logically conceived for generating wisdom from fire and light :

> "O Woman : Eversince the dawn of life
> Thou hast but borne the insults, suffered hard,
> and hast been yet preserving wisdom's light"
> (Book-II, Lines 113-115)

The starting numbers are leapt up with flames when,

> "Mahesh, unburnt, was walking on the flames
> As out he came with Sati's corpse in arms."
> (Book-II, Lines 356-357)

The rage of Mahesh carrying unfumed body of Sati has a superb poetic appeal with everlasting philosophy. The entire journey of Lord Shiva not only signifies man's tragic experience and reconciliation but the reconsummation of human body by PANCHABHUT. The falling parts of Sati create another myth for divine worship while Shiva goes back to Kailash and sits in calm meditation. This calm state of Samadhi has been the highest ideal that mortals can aspire to reach. That is why the poet restrains his pen till he wants to rejoice with the young readers falling in the trap of KAMA, a means to free mankind from earthly sins :

> "If Kama does not come to life, the word
> will die some day. Custodian of the world
> the needs of world demand, my mate should live."
> (Book-IV, Lines, 195-197)

Unfortunately, thematic brilliance is affected by the repetition of the word 'world'. But the rendering of Shiva-Parvati marriage in the heaven produces virtuous elements in Book V and, even today we are to accept.

> "The marriage bonds are forged in Paradise.
> From birth to birth the bonds eternal last,
> Cemented not by senses, but by spirit."
> (Book-V, Lines 386-388)

Then poet adores the fruit of marriage by which Ganesh and Kartikeya are born with wisdom and might though,

"The wisdom and the strength are poles apart
In life where in the youth has strength, not wisdom
While age has wisdom, not the strength..."

(Book-VI, Lines 133-135)

Faith and worship can make us free from YAMA, only then the divine grace can ensure.

"...Glorious triumph of life O'er death."

(Book VII, 400)

It is that enternal story mysteriously adapted in the following Book VIII containing victory of good over evil. Even in the world of mortals, man rages in revolt to fight evils, ordained by faith and moral virtues. This spiritual commentary is quite engrossing and that moves smoothly socio-economic accomplishment of ancient times to justify undeterred discipline. It is tantalizing to visualize Lord Shiva, like the hero of an epic drama, plays the role of a noble king settling all disputes by reconciliations :

"Did Earth allow the air to reach your frame?
Did Earth forsake its share to lend you blood
And flesh and bones?...
Forget you like the thankless future creatures who'll yoke their reasons to their interest mean...
That mother gives us direct, life and food,"

(Book IX, Lines 449-459)

and then Lord Mahesh convinced Kartikeya;

"And deep resentment, Frozen hard by cold
of world's indifference cruel for several years."

(Book-IX, Lines 470-471)

Whatever epic-didacticism has been observed in Book-X, is enough to minimize lust and greed for which man has been suffering since the day of creation. But the divine protagonist consumes all our sins to restore bliss — a search for all times to come. The kingdom of universal bliss is the domain of Lord Shiva. The poet's treatment here seems to have grace in verses combined with the stories of the PURANA ascetically echo the hollowness of power and glory beyond the capacity of the creator and the protector. That is why in Book-XI, the power endowed to Bhasmasur is an end in itself warning the mighty power blocks heading towards inglorious extinction. Glory cannot forge perfection. It requires moral purification to attain completeness, invincible and invisible. The last part of the book depicting fight between Arjuna and Kirat is unmythical, for its sanctifies the goal of man for reaching perfection, the training itself being worship to the high, higher and the highest.

Against the spirituals forestage there sits the mythical God of lust "called *Kaam* exciting all" to understand the endless search for perfection : Reaching the depth of mythical terminology in the narratives, one is tempted to fish in the realm of tacit sex manifested as lusciously as the blooming youth of lascivious young girl just tickling all senses to a vigorous tremour :

> "of bob-cut hair, of breasts exposed and tight,
> .....
> of tapering thighs and upward private parts
> arousing passions base in ogling eyes."
>
> (Book-II, Lines 206-210)

Not extinguished till

> The leaping, dancing, flames around her licked
> Her different parts — the hair, the face, the neck,
> the breast, the waist, the legs, from head to foot —
> And tried their best to lick her down the dust."
>
> (Book-II, Lines 349-352)

and calmed by "...Suckling naked babes on milkful breasts"

(Book-III, Line 96)

This phase of instinct is co-related with the psycho-sexual development in human life. There lies a remarkable credence accurately manoeuvred by a prudent cameraman exposing a good length on a cute for sensational projection of anatomy much applaused to beggar description. What the flesh conspires with the mind is desire in divine when Mahesh says :

> "Your lips are neat-cut mango-slices red
> I'll drink their juice with passionate kisses, love."
>
> (Book-VI, Lines 38-39)

The poet does not consume sex for the element of love of by-gone epochs. It is the race of time that has given births to unrequited love, greed, poverty and unpleasant sex-game. The narrative justifies images of myths mingling with man, energy, life, soul, and sex. This exclusive feature bridges between the fancied existence of paradise and the time-trodden history of all mankind searching bliss through the deserted colonnades of mightiness and psychological hocus pocus, possibly, bringing down the state of man to its lowest ebb. But the continuation of human race, the sinners paradise, cannot be the end by itself. There is an everlasting glory behind the story of creations and the creator. The poet has pulled out true spirits of the narratives from the Purana which through recurrent process still transcend like miracles of the divine. These not only cover legendary myths, but also intensify relations between heaven and earth, evil and good, seat of Lord Shiva by virtue of His authority, rather a vision — an immortal image with which man has been judging good or bad, between revolt and submission or greed and grandeur. The long versification the king of kings attracts lovers of poetry born of argumentative leverage.

The visualizations are philosophical and sublime but without antithesis and balance in the ratiocinations. Gracefully moving from spiritual invocations to the last book of the Rosary. The poet maintains his hunger for a unique style which may find a very high realm of excellence in the future. Other than Indian epics, Milton and Dante, Rosary verses remind me of the mortal verses of Sri Sankaracarya's *Siva Pancashara Stotram*, an example in the heritage of literature.

REFERENCE

Maha Nand Sharma. *A Rudraksha Rosary and other Poems*. Meerut : Ashutosh Prakashan, 1987.

17

Towards a Rise of Consciousness : Humanism in Emerson and Sri Aurobindo (Man *vs.* Society)

—B.C. Dwivedy

"Humanism is an ideal pattern supposed to reveal the true nature of man and the task for which he was born" (Hadas XI). Hadas clarifies that the task of man is shaping himself into a true man thereby creating a society worthy of him to be transmitted to future generation." (Hadas XI)

The society that is perceived in the humanistic thinking is a natural set up in which the existence and liberty of man are not affected, and at the same time, there is a healthy upbringing of man without his submission to the Unknown.

Common interest of individuals gave rise to the formation of what can be said an integrated organism called society which in course of time developed into a state. At the outset there is a shaping of customs, laws, joys and sorrows and all sorts of human affairs. Man is rightly called a social being. Society provides man with a favourable environment for becoming truly human. The cowering and helpless man of pre-historic age has come up to the state of modern man by appropriating power and skill from nature, establishing a need-based kinship with his fellow creatures.

Unity, mutuality and harmony may be regarded as three important principles for any collective life, for promotion of culture, philanthropic welfare, protection of life and growth. The basic factors of a society as C.I. Gulian outlines, may be peaceful co-existence, economic co-operation and exchange of spiritual values (Iyengar, ed., 254). Humanism implies a deep concentration on the awakening, moulding, education and achievement of man's conscience. These factors constitute the personality of man the accomplishment of which is possible only when he performs the social duty in order to achieve a dialectic interaction between the individual and the society.

Modern man is in a state of alienation though an indissoluble coherence between him and his society is the need of the day. As V.N.K. Reddy observes, remedy for the alienation is man's transcendence of his "ego-centric awareness" and "discovery of his real nature" (Reddy, 1973, 287-89). Society helps man to keep his material nature balanced without which he loses his state of equilibrium between matter and spirit. He has to transcend this state and rise towards a greater goal.

Both Emerson and Sri Aurobindo — the transcendental thinkers — have opened new vistas in humanism by extending it to the spiritual need of man and relating it to the functions of society.

Sri Aurobindo believed that when all the actions of the individual are scrupulously regulated by education, law and social machinery what will be achieved is a "regulated pattern of lives and a cultivated pattern of conduct" (Aurobindo, 1993 A, 1022). For this purpose it is necessary for man to change internally and spiritually.

Individual perfection is the basis of the perfection of society. It means the individual's attainment of a divine life through a spiritual fulfilment or in other words, an inner completeness of being which is regarded as the first essential condition of a perfected life. The second condition may be, as Sri Aurobindo observes, the perfection of the spiritual and the pragmatic relation of individual. The third one is a new world, a change in the total life of humanity" *i.e.* a new perfected collective life. (Aurobindo, 1993 A, 1031).

Sri Aurobindo perceives the idea of a "Suprarational age" in which there would be a "deeper brotherhood" and a "yet unfound law of love" that would at as a sure foundation for a perfect social evolution. Such a brotherhood would come in the form of spiritual comradeship" that would mean an "inner realisation of oneness." In other words, a "Spiritualised anarchism" would prevail in the society. It is a spiritual a greater than the rational enlightenment that can alone illumine the vital nature of man, impose harmony on its self-seekings, antagonisms and discords (Aurobindo, 1992, 206). It is not a lawlessness and chaos but a condition in which each individual has the "will to live in harmony with everyone else in the collectivity". (Basu, 1981, 78)

A triple harmony such as harmony within oneself, social harmony between man and man, the harmony between man and the world around him is to be achieved through love of self and love of soul.

> "A bliss, a light, a power, a flame-white love
> Caught all into a sole immense embrace;
>
> Existence found its truth on Oneness breast
> And each became the self and space of all."
>
> ** ** **
>
> All mind was a single harp of many strings
> All life a sony of many meeting lives,
> For worlds were many, but the self was one"
>
> (Aurobindo, 1993 B, 322-23).

Emerson, on the contrary, has emphasised the importance of the individual. However, his uncommon interest in the individual has not affected his opinion on the inevitability of a social surrounding for human upbringing. "A man must be clothed with society" he says, "or we shall feel a certain bareness and poverty as of a displaced and unfurnished member" (Emerson, 1914, "Society and Solitude" 542).

Man in the society is said to be a bundle of relation, "a knot of roots whose flower and fruitage is the world." Man's forces, his attributes and his endowments would have no meaning if they are not applied in a society.

"Put Napoleon in an island prison, let his facilities find no men to act on, no Alps to climb, no stake to play for, and he would beat the air and appear stupid." (Emerson 1926 "History" 77)

Humanists advocate the "primacy of man in everything" and in almost all cases Emerson agrees with them. Sri Aurobindo leads man towards a spiritualised humanism or rather a divine humanism whereas Emerson persists intensively on the side of pure humanism based on human powers, and moves towards a naturalised spirituality "Society is a joint-stock company," he says, "in which the members agree, for the better securing of his bread to each shareholder to surrender the liberty and culture of the eater" (Emerson 1926, 79-80).

Modern faith is liberalism. According to this faith no authoritative code of value is embodied in institutions to guide or discipline man. Man is happy, when he is left most completely free for self-expression. Almost parallel to Sri Aurobindo, Emerson gives the idea of a social surrounding in which the values may be voluntarily adopted by the individual. In such a society there can be a spontaneous growth of a collective power that would make the collective being perfect.

Emerson conceives the idea of a "collective social force", which he says "is powerful in a natural environment and it continues to be powerful, perhaps more powerful in civilised societies."

If all the persons live by the right idea of life to which they have equal access and with the right vision which they can alike share they would shape a pure society.

Emerson also advocates the state of absence of a social machinery, maintenance of a society without artificial restraint. But, it is not through a strictly spiritual or divine transcendence, rather through a natural "reliance on moral sentiment" and "sufficient belief in unity of things." In such a society the principle of "right and love" will be maintained naturally.

Man has co-consciousness or collective consciousness. He lives not with his own individual life but with that of the species. "Once man regains his lost solidarity and consciousness he becomes liberated from fear and acquisitiveness" (Thottackara 99). Therefore, for Aurobindo's "Suprarational state" of society and Emerson's "utopian" society is necessary a rise in collective consciousness which depends on a rise of individual consciousness that can be accomplished through a fulfilment of the spiritual need of man but not essentially a blind submission to the Unknown.

REFERENCES

1. Aurobindo, Sri, *Human Cycle*, Pondicherry, 1992.
2. —— *The Life Divine*, Pondicherry, 1993 A.
3. —— *Savitri*, Pondicherry, 1993 B.
4. Basu, Samar, *Social and Political Evolution of Man*, Pondicherry, 1981.
5. Emerson, R.W., *Essays*, New York, 1914.
6. —— *Emerson's Essays and Poems*, New York, 1926.
7. Hadas, Moses, *The Living Tradition N.P.*, The New American Library, 1967.
8. Iyengar, K.R. Srinivas, ed., *Sri Aurobindo : A Centenary Tribute*, Pondicherry, 1974.
9. Thottackara, Daniel Joseph, Emerson, *The Advatin*, Thevara, 1986.

18

Human Crisis and Superstition in 'Night of the Scorpion'

—*Mrs. Qamar Talat*

Nissim Ezekiel is a modern Indo-Anglian poet for whom India is his motherland. In spite of the fact that he comes of a Jewish parentage, and Jews being the ancient most migrants to India, his emotional attachment to India and the manner in which he celebrates his Indianism in his poetry is in itself a matter of intense devotion towards the country as a whole. That way Ezekiel is a modern poet with a sort of skeptical attitude towards the emotional factors in life, including love. But, however, there are innumerable poems of Ezekiel which go to celebrate India in innumerable ways. Depending upon his mood sometimes he is devotional as in 'In India,' sometimes he is intensely passionate about its ancestry and tradition as in 'Background Casually' yet sometimes he is critical of its age worn traditions, faiths and beliefs as in 'Night of the Scorpion.' In an over all manner he expresses a typical disgust at the backwardness and at the unfeeling nature of Indian society. Therefore for an objective observation the life styles in India offer incongruities in themselves; and thereby presenting India as a land of immensely laughable dimensions. Therefore Ezekiel involves himself with India and its Indianism in such a critical manner that it all becomes a profound satire on the back looking Indians and their orthodox traditions and operations.

Nissim Ezekiel's poem 'Night of the Scorpion' is a very interesting poem which presents the popular superstition of the

Indian masses. As a matter of fact there is no rational manner of understanding or withstanding the problem here. R. Taranath and M. Belliappa characterized the poem as :

> The observer's neutral attitude to the scene, balancing the superstitions with the presence of the father, 'sceptic, rationalist,' makes the supernatural a poetically credible quantity in an episode which stands transformed into an experience of significance, at least to the believers.

Scorpions stinging the people is a very common phenomena in the suburban areas of India. Scorpion is a tropical pest; and the pain of its sting is in itself quite unbearable physically as well as mentally. In the context of the poem the mother in the family was stung by a scorpion. Quite naturally she is restless and suffers from acute pain. Out of this situation Ezekiel humorously brings out a typical ironic manner of the attending agents in treating the patient. This poem can be taken as one of the finest example of black humour. Instead of going for some sort of rationally approved pain killer, all the relatives and the attending neighbours resort to all sorts of superstitions and propositions of curing. In fact, it is the mother of the protagonist that received the sting. To that extent the protagonist's child-like emotional agitations and anxieties are understandable. But, in the presence of the superstitions of advisers, which includes his rationalist father also, he becomes a mere mute observer trying to contain the pain of his mother silently and sympathetically in himself. But the protagonist is conscious of the absurdity ruling the roost in the situation. There is a tendency among Indians to consider any sort of pain as a metaphysical formula of reminding people about the needful other worldly philosophy of life they must ultimately evolve for themselves. Pain, according to the back looking Indian philosophy should become a sort of reminder for the people in order to make them resigned from the desires in this life. They also believe that it is through pain only that man becomes purified. Hence :

> The peasants came like swarms of flies and buzzed
> the Name of God a hundred times to paralyse the Evil
> One.

This is the height of their superstition and unwithstandable at that in taking the 'Name of God' hundred times to ward off the 'Evil One.' One has a significant reference to Christian metaphor throughout also. The repercussion of the fight between God and Satan in the Christian mythology targeting man as the sufferer in itself is an absurd metaphysics. Indians are also equally God-fearing. It is this sense of God-fear that makes them conscious for themselves a typical altruistic philosophy of life. Indians particularly believe in re-incarnation. Therefore, they tried to console the patient :

> May the sins of your previous birth be burned
> away tonight, they said.
> May your suffering decrease the misfortunes of
> your next birth, they said.
> May the sum of evil balanced in this unreal world
> against the sum of good become diminished by
> your pain.

From the practical scorpion the streak of imagination transcendencing to innumerable births and deaths is in itself ridiculous and absurd. But nobody can help it. Such is the extend of poverty of imagination. In pronouncing :

> May the poison purify your flesh
> of desire, and your spirit of ambition.
> They said, and they sat around
> on the floor with my mother in the centre,
> the peace of understanding on each face.

The poet is the only person who is emotionally concerned in watching 'the flame feeding on my mother.' Ultimately the holy men tried to 'tame the poison with an incantation.' We have here all the paraffinoid of mystic cures and metaphysical advices. It is very difficult to know whether the father's act of 'putting a match' to the bitten toe aggravated the pain or lessened it. In spite of the fact that he is a rationalist his act in the present context definitely contributed for more pain being added to the already unbearable pain of the mother. Quite naturally :

> After twenty hours
> it lost its stings.

The poem expressionistically presents innumerable vollies of structural strokes. But the end stroke is quite interesting and humorous :

> My mother only said
> Thank God the Scorpion picked on me and
> spared my children.

Innumerable critics pointed out that the sting itself is "a symbol of evil." This concept of reading evil in the context makes a holistic stride towards apprehending the aesthetics of evil, in the Christian context. There is a way of reading this poem as a ridiculous parody of the 'Book of Job' in the *Holy Bible.* M.K. Naik in his article on Ezekiel 'The Tale is in the Sting' says that :

> It would, therefore, be more appropriate to characterize the basic theme of the poem as the mystery of Evil and the enigma of the suffering attendant upon it.

The biblical analogy here is quite casual and non-serious. Therefore, it is a light-hearted parody. The mystery of evil and enigma of suffering attended upon it are in themselves suggestive of the metaphysical dimensions reached by Ezekiel in quite a humorous manner. It is just possible that he is trying to laugh at the absurd conceptual formulas of evils both in the Christianity and in the eastern religions. Hence 'Night of the Scorpion' remains an interesting and very valid poem, containing a fascinating tension between personal crisis and mocking social observation.

19

Orientalism in Nissim Ezekiel

—*A.A. Khan*

Nissim Ezekiel is one of the most respected of the living Indian poets writing in English. Nissim Ezekiel, having the background of Ben-Israels, has opted India as his homeland. This fact speaks of Nissim Ezekiel's Indianness. From time immemorial India has been the meeting ground of different cultures and creeds, and yet she has the power of assimilating the divergent currents and undercurrents into the mainstream. Ezekiel's Jewish background and his assimilation into Indian mainstream verifies the old Indian saying that the whole universe is a brotherhood. Centuries of oppression and humiliation have resulted in persecution mania and fear psychosis among the Jews who could find a congenial homeland in India as in the case of Nissim Ezekiel. However, his Jewish background finds expression in his prayer to God :

> Kick me around
> a bit more, O Lord.[1] (JSAL, 133)

This prayer is quite different from the traditional prayer of Indian bowing before the Almighty and Merciful God. Yet, Ezekiel has typical characteristics of Indianness to be one with the confluence of mainstream. Instead of being a world citizen, Ezekiel opted to be an Indian and to be deep-rooted in Indian soil where thousand flowers bloom involving the all-comprehensive, all-embracing spirit of Indianness. In reply to a questionaire, Nissim Ezekiel affirmed to be an Indian because "he did not want to be rootless."[2] Ezekiel's ancestors were 'oil seed pressers.' In Indian tradition Saturday is the day of Saturn or 'Shani' who is appeased by the offering of oil on Saturday. Bene-Israels took to oil pressing soon after arrivals in India. Hence Shanwar Teli, oil presser caste, Ezekiel refers to his ancestors :

> My ancestors, among the castes, were aliens crushing
> seed for bread. (The hooded bullock made his rounds.)
>
> (JSAL, 86)

"The hooded bullock" is the traditional symbol of dull routine and drudgery. It is peculiarly reminiscent of good old leisurely days. The nomenclature 'Shanwar teli' — Saturday oil pressers is not merely based on superstition about 'Shani', but an inner urge to be one with the myths and traditions without being blind believers in unfounded beliefs.

The title "A Time to Change" has significant meaning beyond the literal meaning. Ernest Hemingway in the first quarter of the twentieth century named his collection of short stories "In Our Time", the title being taken from the Common Prayer Book. Ezekiel, imbibing the spirit of fifties of the twentieth century along with the renaissance spirit in Indian sub-continent, has faith in himself as in the whole mankind to cope with the time to change himself to lead the world in the realm of liberty, equality and fraternity. India on the threshold of independence has the realisation to break the felters of conversation and fundamentalism to breathe fresh air in an environment where head is held high and mind is in the ever-widening circle of knowledge. The title "A Time to Change" reflects the spirit of the whole age.

Nissim Ezekiel resided mostly in Bombay and in constant touch with the elite society of sophisticated people, yet he has instinctive sympathy with the rural population representating in its own way the spirit of real India. Ezekiel is in touch with the common people also. Kabir, the famous saintly poet, sang of the throes of the downtrodden people, and exploded the myth of ritualistic religion. Kabir's famous lines :

> *Lakri jal bhaee koela,*
> *Koela jal bhaee rakh,*
> *Mein Papan aisi jali,*
> *na koela bhaee na rakh.*[3]

often sung by his devotees, have found expression in Nissim Ezekiel's poem :

> I know that wood if burnt
> Produces ash and smoke
> There is law about this, explaining
> How and where the burnt wood went.
>
> (JSAL, 48)

Kabir's lines are in praise of love which 'breaks the incendiary laws.' In Kabir's poem the singer is a woman and Ezekiel's poem is titled *For Her*. (JSAL, 48)

Almost imperceptively Ezekiel has imbibed the spirit of 'Qawwali' in some of his early and latter poems. 'Qawwali' is sung by a group of singers in cordant notes, the music being supplied by the rhythmic clapping. The 'Sufi' saints used Qawwali as a mass media for inculcating the moral virtues. The hearers are often in a state of trance when the burthen of the mystery of life become clear and they become living soul to understand the unintelligible world. In Qawwali the rhythmic movement of stanzas has the sublimating effect by the repetition of the same line. In Nissim Ezekiel's poems the influence of Qawwali is clearly visible. The poem "Two Nights of Love" has two stanzas of six lines each. The opening line of the first stanza is :

> After a night of love, I dreamt of love (JSAL, 31)

The opening line of the second stanza has slight variation :

> After a night of love, I turned to love. (JSAL, 31)

Last two lines of the first stanza are repeated with slight variation in the last two lines of the second stanza.

The poem "The Stone" has the technique akin to that of Qawwali. The opening line is :

> I have learnt to revel in the stone, (JSAL, 25)

The second stanza also begins with :

> I have learnt to love the texture of stone, (JSAL, 25)

The last line of the first stanza is :

> Not to be caressed, like flesh, but hard as
> bone. (JSAL, 25)

The second stanza ends with :

> But shares its nature like the hidden bone. (JSAL, 25)

The poem "Old Abyss" (JSAL, 31) is in two stanzas. The second stanza is the exact reproduction of the first one. The repetition leaves the hearers in a sublime mood when he is lifted out of himself. Ezekiel says :

> Not the words that are found
> But the singing counts. (JSAL, 49)

Finally Ezekiel says :

> And now I hear the first birds
> Spasmodic and repetitive...
> I know I shall repeat myself. (JSAL, 49)

The oriental attitude is of complete surrender to the will of God. In the poem "Planning," everything was done to the best of knowledge;

> Relying only on the skilful hand,

however the things went wrong because the planners,

> Allowed for everything except a long
> Arresting arm, the unseen, the Unknown. (JSAL, 24)

Nissim Ezekiel has become the part and parcel of philosophy of despair, leading to Indian passivity, detachment and acceptance — "India is simply my environment," (JSAL, 203) says Nissim Ezekiel. Modesty, humility and self-effacement are the abiding qualities of Indian temperament.

> I have made my commitments now,
> This is one : to stay where I am,
> As others choose to give themselves
> In some remote and backward place.
> My backward place is where I am. (JSAL, 86)

Nissim Ezekiel is perfectly satisfied with "backward place." It is the modesty of a typical Indian. Finally Nissim Ezekiel prays to God :

Confiscate my passport, Lord,
I don't want to go abroad.
Let me find my song
Where I belong.

REFERENCES

1. The abbreviation used is JSAL — *Journal of South Asian Literature*, Guest Editor — Inder Nath Kher, *Nissim Ezekiel Issue*, Volume XI, Spring, Summer, 1976, Numbers 3-4 (Asian Studies Center, Michigan State University, East Lansing, Michigan, 1976).

2. Anisur Rehman, *Form and Value in the Poetry of Nissim Ezekiel* (Abhinav Publication, New Delhi, 1981), p. 36.

3. *Kabir Granthawali*, p. 97.

20

The First Milestone : A Critique of Sinha's *Harbour Lights*

—Asha Choubey

A compact collection of imagery and colours, dreams and disillusionments, of aspirations and expectations, of futility and hopes and of experiences and visions has got the name — *Harbour Lights*. The title suits the poem as well as the collection like a glove as the collection telescopes the kaleidoscopic observations of the sensitive poet just as — to borrow the words of the poet — harbour lights 'Telescopes the stars into a tunnel.' Unless one reads the information given on the back, one would not believe that this is the first collection from Sinha's pen. So wide is the poet's horizon and so intense in his sensitivity that one could finish the whole book at one go, without ever feeling a bit of monotony. The poet has a keen observation and his interest is varied — including within its spectrum such light subjects as *The Spice Girls* to those of such magnitude — *Dreams, Change* and *The Birth*. The characteristic that makes the difference, however is Sinha's contemplative propensity.

The poet seems to possess a special inclination towards imagery. The images drawn by Dr. Sinha are fresh in their appeal. A particularly attractive picture that has been haunting me since is from the poem *Morning* :

> The sun in yellow turban
> Bends low to kiss
> His sleeping bride awake, (21)

It's a picture that is oven-fresh and yet breeds nostalgia, conveying not only the pictorial beauty of morning but also its emotional piety and its festivity. The picture of the bride becomes complete in the next lines :

> Cornfields sway to anklet music
> Rills smile pearls. (*Ibid.*)

Anklet and pearls build up the mood of celebration. *Secret* is a three-line beautiful poem exemplifying the poet's skill in imagery :

> Trees bring heads
> Together in a green whisper
> Sharing secrets. (25)

Such lovely pictures are scattered all through the collection. The poet has an eye for senses. There is seldom or never a noun without an adjective preceding it and more often than not the adjective is one of colour : blue skies (*To a Child in a Bombed City*), white bones and mudbrown ponds (*Famine*), yellow ground; white page and shades of blue and grey (*Seedless*), green whisper (*Secret*) and orange light (*A Political Rally*) are only some examples. The poems in this collection have a Keatsian appeal in the quality of sensuousness to senses is concerned and present a feast specially for the sense of sight, touch and smell.

> Soft fingers,
> Cool and hennaed,
> Touch-tired eyes. (*Dusk*)
> And
> Wet palms warm with blood
> Throbbing like distant drums
> In a rain forest
> Hold your hands. (*Change*)
> And
> ... neatly stacked lights
> Feel the cold lips of rain (*Harbour Lights*)

Present lovely instances of the sense of touch.

> Only the smell of crushed flowers,
> And young bodies in silk
> Lingers. (*Encounter At Mathura*)

And

The stench must end-
It must be funny to watch
An entire nation marching into the future
With the handkerchief to its nose.

(*Fifty Years of Independence*)

And

The air is heavy with incense
And the smell of clothes freshly starched.

(*Encounter At Mathura*)

And

Dusk descends
And covers frail earth
With tresses that smell
Of rose and mischief. (*Dusk*)

Offer satisfaction to olfactory nerves.

The river has moved close to my house,
Every night I hear
Its insane whisper. (*Defence*)

And

The glass-lit chrome stage
Is a whirlwind of sound.
Blood beats time
As freshly plucked music
Piles on the ground. (*The Spice Girls*)

And

The breeze whispers old stories,
Remembered and forgotten. (*Dusk*)

And

We have rushed into the mire
Of frayed dreams where the fire's demented laughter
Fills the night.
All night we have been singing a mad song,

(*In a New Country*)

Bring a varied spectrum of sounds to mind.

Sinha's poems bring to mind Mill's observation : What is poetry, but the thought and words in which emotion spontaneously embodies itself ? (Thoughts on Poetry and its Varieties, in dissertations and discussions, vol. i.) It is remarkable, however that his spontaneity brings forward lines which have a perfect finish as well. A perfect combination of polish and spontaneity may be seen is the lines from *My Lost Poem* :

A familiar winter fills my room,
My untitled poem lies somewhere on this cold floor
Littered with crumpled words.

Not one word leaves the possibility of substitution. Similarly the opening lines of *Fifty Years of Freedom* are an example non-pareil :

In the desert of empty abstractions
Died the dreams,
The days fractured, the mornings jaundiced,
We have come a long way
From the fragrance of rain forests.

The disillusionment, the sense of waste have been deftly conveyed through the images. While jaundiced mornings represent pale hopes and wrong beginnings; fractured days convey impotent strength and invalid ideas.

If brevity is the soul of wit, Sinha again stands the winner. In the collection almost all the poems are short and brief, though they contain volumes of emotions. *Fifty Years of Freedom* is the only long poem in the book, rest are 3-4 stanza poems. But the poems which are really remarkable for their meaningful brevity are the three-liners — *Dreams, Faces* and *Secret*. The imagery in these poems leaves nothing unsaid :

A bird rises
Straight up into the sky,
The earth chases dreams. (*Dreams*)

The fleeting transience of dreams dominates the atmosphere here. This is true of *Secret* as well :

Trees bring heads
Together in a green whisper
Sharing secrets.

These poems are word-pictures which act as the 'objective

correlative' for the ideas making them concretely vivid before the reader's eyes. The word-pictures of Sinha make these ideas so clear and understandable as they had never been. How correct was Browning when he wrote :

> For don't you mark ? We're made so that we love
> First when we see them painted, things we have pass'd
> Perhaps a hundred times, nor cared to see;
> And so they are better, painted — better to us,
> Which is the same thing. Art was given for that. (*Fra Lippo Lippi*)

Sinha emerges as a keen observer and has his eyes and ears open for all that forms his milieu. The very first poem in the collection — *To a Child in a Bombed City* stands a brilliant example to this. The horror of war and the destruction and calamity are encapsulated in this short poem which evokes emotion without lapsing into melodramatics. This has been made possible by Sinha's skill in drawing images and his perfect word-choice. The picture of a child cuddling against his mother's warm form, brings to mind innocence searching for security. But the 'scorched womb' highlights on one hand the fact that under such horrible circumstances even security has been rendered insecure, exposed to dangers; and on the other hand womb being the source of life, it also signifies the end of all life at its very source — a total despair. Similarly 'your night was ripped' conveys the shattering of peace. Night and evening have been presented as time for peace and rest. The repetition of 'for ever' in the closing lines makes it subtly clear that the wait for life, for innocence shall become unending if these 'eyeless missiles' are allowed to deposit 'boiling light' at the doorstep of innocence.

At the Golconda Fort shows the poet's ability to breathe life into dead history, to feel the agony and the pain that have seldom been voiced as feelingly as here :

> The narrator's voice rings
> In roofless corridors,
> Scab words fall
> From the wounds of Golconda.

Your Poets, Famine and *A Political Rally* present the irony of the present system.

> Waves of high pressured political creed
> Assail you.
> Why do so many join
> The festival demented phrases?

The sense of aimlessness and insanity of politically motivated men conveyed here is typical of the scene in Bihar (home state of the poet) though West Bengal and U.P. may well compete. *Famine* to my mind is one of the best and the most ironical of poems written on the subject. Without indulging in rhetoric, the poet unearths the irony. "Parched villages wait/ For their allocated share/ of official sympathy," seems to mock the mechanical sympathy that is hurled at the victims. Allocated share and official sympathy are phrases full of meaning and convey the artificiality of kindness and calculated concern shown to the famine victims. For politicians famine comes as yet another opportunity to gain political mileage :

> Famine is news,
> Seminars will be organized, speeches made,
> Old scores settled, political gains calculated;
> Pain never sold so well.

In *Your Poets* the poet exposes the politicians who look down upon poets as mere intellectuals, incapable of action. It brings to light the impotence the powers that be. Poets are put on a high platform :

> The roads you walk on
> Go past the battlefields.
> Stand aside, my friend, and watch
> Some crazy men fight your battles for you;
> They are your poets.

Coleridge once wrote : "No man was ever yet a great poet without being at the same time a profound philosopher." (*Biographia Literaria*, ch. xv) Sinha proves this true with his contemplative bent of mind as evinced in poems like *The Birth, The Pyre Song* and *Seedless*. The latter brings out the impotence of man before the horrors of life and the futility of his efforts to bring harmony :

> I have no more poems to write,
> The virgin white page
> All smeared with confused
> Shades of blues and greys.
> Seedless I stand on the edge of day
> And stare at the wrinkled face of earth.

The philosopher in Sinha peeps through the lines from *The Pyre Song* :

> It's time to cross water again,
> It's time to take off your tattered days.
> The Ganga is red at this raddled hour,
> The winds hurry to take you home.

Death is seen as a home coming of the soul that has wandered for long. While life is tedious, death is a balm which brings relief to the "tattered days."

Evening has been presented as a harbinger of peace and hope, contrary to its traditional portrayal :

> Peace will come eventually,
> As the last rays of the sun
> Stream through leaves
> Waiting for death. (*Evening Thoughts*)

The setting of sun has been traditionally associated with hopelessness, despair, gloom and even death. But Sinha associates it with peace, life, desire and even birth :

> In the glow of the hibiscus evening,
> And in the hush of longing,
> A poem is born. (*The Birth*)

Our Enlightenment is a satire on materialistic approach. Siddhartha had all material pleasures at his disposal but he gave up everything for the sake of pursuing knowledge. But those were another days and another times. We do not have to undertake difficult journey towards enlightenment because our definition of the same is different. The modern Buddha does not have to take to a life of austerity as he is after worldly wisdom that comes easy and swift. The modern Buddha does not need to conquer his desires, instead he gives them full rein. Lust and wealth have become the order of the day :

How effortless has been
Our enlightenment!
Desires do not breed grief;
Watered with wealth and lust,
They flower into instant wisdom.
Come, and look at us,
O Prince of Kapilvastu!

Meeting is a simple poem about meeting and parting. Meeting brings some moments of 'great security' but there is one relief — that there is no commitment. Commitments also leave memory behind which keeps ripping the heart. Hence, the best option is to come and go unremembered without leaging behind footprints :

It was nice of you to come
And leave
Nothing behind.

Fifty Years of Freedom forces one to ponder over the present state of anarchy, terror and ethical degeneration :

We smear our foreheads with bone-dust
As the worship of the self
Continues in the city of cacophony.

Our lives, our values are all moth-eaten and we refuse to acknowledge the irony of our existence. The poet despises such false sense of well-being and security when all our dreams are burning. An ostrich-like safety will not help. In order that the wounds may be cured, they must first be diagnosed. It's high time we stopped cherishing delusions and deceptions :

A malignant life it is,
We have closed our eyes
To the terror that darkens the landscape.
It is a world peopled
With thousand hallucinations of greatness.

The poet as a responsible citizen invokes the countrymen :

It is time to come out
Of our private winters,
And shake off our curse.
Let the gress grow again
In this desert.
Let the sunflower
Converse with the confident sun,
Once again.

If one were to choose a single word that may describe the collection, I think 'variegated' would be the best choice. The poet presents not only a variety of form, subject, similes, analogies and atmosphere but also presents them with equanimity of style and with utmost ease. Nothing seems out of his range of experience, nothing is alien or new. Though this is the first anthology of his poems, the name of Dr. Sinha is not new to us. Many of the poems have appeared in other journals at different times and they have successfully whetted our appetite for some more. We have all reasons to hope that this harbour is only the beginning of a long, flourishing voyage across the sea of poetry and that there are many more harbours to come *en route*. An encounter with *Harbour Lights* is naturally a pleasant meeting but happily it does leave something behind (unlike the meeting in his poem) — promises of even more such lights to be generated from the poet's pen.

REFERENCE

Sinha, Ravi Nandan, 1998. *Harbour Lights*, Ranchi : Writers Forum. (All references are to this edition).

LIST OF CONTRIBUTORS

O.P. Bhatnagar is a renowned poet and critic of Indian Writing in English. He is the author of a large number of papers. He has been to many Asian and European countries participating in poetry conferences.

R.A. Singh is a Professor and Head, S.P. Jain College, Sasaram (Veer Kunwar Singh University, ARA). He is the author of two dozen books and similar number of research papers.

P. Raja is Professor of English, Tagore Arts College, Pondicherry. He is a well-known poet and critic, author of a dozen books.

G.D. Barche is Reader, Department of English, S.S.V.P.S. Arts and M.F. M.A. Com. College, Dhule (M.S.). He has contributed a large number of papers on Indian and British literature. He is a renowned practitioner of yoga.

D.C. Chambial, Heads the Department of English, Govt. P.G. College, Palampur (HP). He edits *Poetcrit*, an International Journal of Poetry and Criticism. He is also a poet and a critic.

D. Gnanasekaran is Reader in English in a college in Pondicherry. He has many critical papers to his credit.

K.V. Raghupathi is a well-known critic of Indian Poetry in English. He is an established critic.

Sanjay Mukherjee is on the Faculty of English, Saurashtra University, Rajkot. He is a promising writer and critic.

B.P. Sinha is on the Faculty of English, Ranchi University, Ranchi. He is associated with Akashvani and Doordarshan, Ranchi. He has made a film which is very popular on the screen.

Birendra Pandey, Heads the Department of English, B.S. College, Hatta (Chenari), Rohtas. He is the author of the book *The Novels of Arun Joshi : A Critical Evaluation.* He has edited two anthologies : *Indian Poetry in English* and Recent *Women Novelists in Indian Writing in English.*

Vinod Kumar Singh, Lecturer in H.C.P.G. College, Varanasi (U.P.).

T. Raghavan is Retired Professor of English, S.V. Arts College, Tirupati. At present he is engaged in creative writing and criticism on poetry and fiction. He lives at Tirupati.

Kumari Vibha Agrawal teaches at a college at Raipur (MP). She has her Ph.D. on the poetry of Dr. O.P. Bhatnagar. She is a promising creative writer.

P.S. Radha is in the Department of English, St. Joseph's College, Irinjalakuda, Kerala.

M.K. Pandey, Heads the Department of English, Hindu Degree College, Zamania, Ghazipur (U.P.).

V.K. Arora is Senior Lecturer, Department of English, Government Degree College, Ajmer, Rajasthan.

B.C. Dwivedy is at K.V. Dhenkanal, Orissa.

Mrs. Qamar Talat is Asst. Prof. of English, Govt. Arts and Science College, Durg (M.P.).

A.A. Khan is Asst. Prof. of English, Govt. College, Utai, Durg (M.P.).

Dr. Asha Choubey, Lecturer, Kanya Mahavidyalya, Bareilly.